The Descent of the God
The Continuing Incarnation

by
Lorna M. Marsden

Sessions Book Trust
York, England

ISBN 1 85072 093 2

Printed on recycled paper in 10 on 11 point Plantin Typeface
by William Sessions Limited
The Ebor Press, York, England

Contents

Preface

THE DESCENT OF THE GOD IS A FORM of expression for that central human experience by which the idea of divinity has seemed inseparable from the human condition. Even in moments of its eclipse – as now – this idea is not altogether extinguished. Behind the contemporary preoccupation with the analytical and synthesising faculties of the mind, and the allurements of an almost totally externalised life, there lies at this moment a deep uneasiness. This has, perhaps, two sources. One source is that of the opening horizons of science upon greatly expanded ideas of the workings of both matter and the cosmos, and the repercussions of these ideas on the texture of human thought – both in relation to all that has followed on the splitting of the atom, and to the question of spirituality. The other source is the increasing realisation that the ecological, economic, and political disorders of the world, its increasing cruelties and dangers, are becoming intolerable. We are threatened by the possible extinction of ourselves, our civilisation, and our planet.

It is in this situation that the West is experiencing the slow but steady permeation of society by the rise of a movement towards radical change. This change involves a reappraisal of the nature of human responses, particularly in relation to religious meaning.

The ideas of religion and of art make use of the language of imagery, of the forms of painting and sculpture, of the harmonies of music, to express those fundamental experiences which lie behind and beneath the superficial workings of the brain, and which are common to the trained and the untrained human being alike. Even in the hour of their apparent decline they still exist underground, for they are inseparable from the state of human *being*.

The cultivation of a separated, purely discursive intellect for its own sake has been the obsession of our times. In its close relation to the achievements of mathematics it has given us those remarkable artefacts, instruments, and exploratory techniques which have been the particular mark of our brilliantly inventive era. However, the unbalanced cultivation of these approaches has led us also into the cul-de-sacs of positivism and reductionism, which neglect the intuitive, visionary aspects of human experience. This has contributed to the setting in motion of a rejection of

iv

organised religion, thus obscuring that religious meaning which is not dependent on possibly outmoded institutions. A kind of infection from such attitudes has often bowdlerised and dessicated the arts, and has evoked nihilism. Our world has been thrown into a confusion that appears a-moral and suicidal. There has been created a frantic worship of material acquisition, of speed of travel, and of total exploitation both of the many by the few and of our planet. Human beings have produced the means of mutual destruction, and sanctioned the hoarding of such means.

But, by the bringing of all the regions of the world nearer together, the whole of humanity has also been faced with the spectacle of its own condition of danger and disorder, and there has been evoked at last a growing revulsion. Although the new directions of science, particularly of experimental physics, has been instrumental in the achievement of this revulsion, coincidental with this has been the re-evaluation of spirituality seen no longer as discardable by the self-motivated and limited 'cleverness' of mankind, but as crucial to a fulfilled life. Or perhaps these parallel movements of change are something more than coincidental. The newest theories of systems science will tell us that disequilibrium is itself the catalyst of change. In the extremity of mankind's present disequilibrium is the same process at work and saving change truly imminent? Such change involves a re-assessment of the derogated powers of the mind and a new conception of human wholeness.

The expression of the idea of incarnation belongs to these devalued powers. It uses the language of myth – of metaphor. Myth and metaphor cover those aspects of human experience which cannot be expressed by the processes of ratiocination. Whether articulated or not, such experiences are basic to the human condition. Since their images derive from the common human unconscious, they are recognisable by all men and women. Where they are neglected or defamed life sinks. The ebb of an inner vitality supervenes, and we are caught in that fragmentation of human life which has been our contemporary condition.

In the intoxication aroused by our apparent conquest of the outer world it has been forgotten that the powerful movement of feeling and of imaginative response has its own disciplines, which are the fount of our inner and essential vitality. Within these disciplines the intuitive insights of mankind function creatively. They do so out of the unconscious depths of the mind in forms recognisable to all within a particular culture, and – increasingly – beyond that.

One such form is the idea of incarnation. Today, we have the possibility of a conscious extension of the area of its meaning. We stand on the verge of a re-evaluation both of the inner life of mankind as the matrix of all creative outward action, and – from within science itself – of a new vision of the cosmos. All these things are considerations which arise within the context of the continuing incarnation.

CHAPTER I

Change and the Tradition

THROUGHOUT RECORDED HISTORY, THE HUMAN JOURNEY appears to have been shadowed by a sense of provisionality, and a sense also of *accompaniment* – as though humanity's realisation of itself required an endorsement of its actuality from beyond itself, in order that it should not dissolve upon the empty air. We are told that certain primitive tribes have even gone so far as to see their own existence as something dreamed by a remote and inaccessible dreamer. Who shall say today that those who live within this attitude deserve the name of 'primitive'?

One thing at least is clear. From out of that almost total externalisation of our life which has preoccupied contemporary Western man – from under the shadow of those remarkable artefacts which have accented this preoccupation – there is emerging a renewed sense, not only of an unresolved mystery in our existence but also of an awareness of an essential significance in the neglected, the almost derided, inner life of mankind. This inner life is the life of the imagination and the soul, which has given us not only a sense of what we call God, but has also given us the divinations of all forms of art, and of the experiences of love and compassion. Against the tide of the times a new evaluation of these things is already discernible. Also contributory to this revival have been the latest explorations of science which have penetrated both the insubstantiality of matter and the relativities of time and space.

Following closely on the end of the era of ancient Greece, there arose within the civilised world a new conception, of which Christianity was one element. The implacability of Fate was broken. There became open to the human mind the possibility of choice, of inner freedom. Within both Buddhism and Christianity, this element of choice was mediated not simply by reason but also by the opening out of the power of the human spirit as a whole. What Christianity specifically offered was a new conception of the meaning of suffering and of vulnerability. The doctrine of incarnation in its Christian form was a part of this change.

The figure of Jesus as prophet and as archetypal myth is unassailable. Yet the figure of Jesus as an historically unique incarnation of the divine is

1

no longer generally accepted in a literal sense. Today, church writers are themselves producing contorted disputations in an attempt to face this issue.

As presented in the New Testament the teaching of Jesus releases us from slavery to the moral law, from the tyranny of a self-sufficient rationality, and from an interpretation of the human world in terms that are abstractions. He speaks directly to the human heart in its day-to-day experiences. He sees God in personal terms. He suffers, is angry, is filled with pity and forgiveness. He speaks, not of belief and codes of conduct, but of faith – and for him the supreme expression of faith is the action of love. These things speak to us with power, and will go on doing so while his name remains with us.

Yet, for orthodox Christianity, these things are set in the context of a greater claim. It is the outlines of this greater claim which, emerging from the shadows of the past, are becoming extended and illumined by the increasing brightening of the human consciousness. This light of human self-awareness crosses the frontiers of the past, so that the archetypal figure of Jesus Christ is seen, not as set for ever in the distant land of Galilee or the ancient city of Jerusalem, but as moving within us. In so moving, he points us forward towards an extended awareness of what may be meant by the entrance of the divine into the world. But in pointing us forward he also points us back.

This process began when the early church identified the Jesus of history with the Greek Logos. Whatever the blindnesses, the mistakes, and the exclusivity of the church from that time on, this was the beginning of what we face now. The horizon of meaning was opened, even if that opening was curtained off. It was curtained off when the church became hierarchically organised and therefore limited. The opening is still there today, and the curtain is swinging apart.

We remember the first words of St John's gospel: 'In the beginning was the Word, and the Word was with God, and the Word was God.' Where this Word is made flesh in him who was called the Son of God, truth is felt, not as a mental structure, but as an encounter. Later, the incarnation of the Word was to be seen by some who called themselves Christian not as a single historical event but as a continually repeated event within the soul.

Heretical to the church, historically this insight goes very far back, and was voiced by various individuals down the centuries. In the religious ferment of the 17th century particularly it was advanced by radical Christians in England, and crystallised in the formation of the Quaker faith, (where it is still found today, in contrast to the attitudes of the institutionalised churches).

And now, in our day? – In considering the idea of incarnation as continuing in the context of our own times, are we coming to a watershed of

2

changed directions as great as that where, at a particular moment of history, the Jewish Messiah was assimilated to the Greek conception of the Logos? At that point, the historical Jesus became lost – or found – according to how you look at it – as the second Person of the Trinity, a conceptualisation in which his concreteness was transformed. Today, the signs of great, even of drastic, change are everywhere, and they point to a rejection of the projection of our need for salvation on to a quasi-historical figure. (Nevertheless, his meaning has entered into the consciousness of our inner life – and perhaps into the forms of our social life.)

But the contemporary movement towards a rejection of the theological conceptualisation of Jesus is not in itself new – as already suggested. It is interesting and instructive to follow some of those precursors of Quakerism who, through the centuries of church history acted as gadflies to orthodoxy, and were condemned as heretics. For they saw behind the idea of incarnation, not the structures of reasoned doctrine or the limitations of the edifice of power that was the church, but an image of the human condition whose truth is central to the experience of mankind. It is the validity of this image of the entry of the divine into the human which makes possible in our own day the expansion of the incarnational vision. For the power of imagery expresses depths that are inaccessible to reasoned thought, but are plastic to time and history.

The sense of the provisional mentioned earlier, and the sense that somehow in the struggles of life we are accompanied by the god (or the angel) has been focused in the West on the figure of Jesus Christ as the promise of fulfilment and the form of hope. For what haunts a humanity awakened to a new consciousness of its own possibilities is the remembrance of Paradise. (This too is an imagery open to the changes of time and history.)

For what is meant by the provisional except the sense that haunts mankind of being in exile? – and by an awareness of accompaniment except the consciousness of the presence of the Other, who among the visionaries of the world, takes many forms? For the poet Rilke, as for the biblical Jacob, and many others, it was the Angel. For the Sufi, who recognises the twofold nature of identity, it is the image of his own Lord, the Angel who is his divine counterpart. For the mountaineer, it is another presence at the moment of danger or of heightened anticipation. For the contemporary neurologist it is the detached observer watching the actions of the individual from within. For the Nakapi of Labrador, it is the internal 'friend' whose departure signals death.[1]

We are conscious that within and about us there is more than ourselves. This we know, not by reason, but on the pulse of our living experience. In

[1] Alex Comfort: *I and That, Notes on the Biology of Religion*. Michael Beazley Ltd., 1979.

3

the inner spaces of our own being we encounter this 'more'. Our externalised, self-worshipping civilisation has tried to ignore this. Yet it may well be the only true fount of our vitality, even of our viability as human beings. To begin to recognise this situation may be the condition of our redemption from world suicide.

Rejection of the way that institutionalised religion presents itself – endemic now in most of the Western community – does not justify to the intelligence rejection of those basic intuitions by which every religious attitude was originally shaped. Just as wholesale rejection of the Bible, apparently justified by its contradictions, its sometimes primitive and barbaric attitudes, its non-literal history, etc., becomes an act of indefensible crudity which destroys the essential hermeneutics by which mankind maps the route of its advance. At various levels response to what lies below the surface appearance of biblical narrative and biblical poetry have formed our civilisation. These things are as native to the cast of our minds, and more widespread, as the classical scholarship with which they have shared a curious alliance. Rejections that are blind are worthless. It is not rejection that we need but that kind of understanding by which we recognise in what now seem the excesses of the past not only the seeds of the future, but in the midst of a chaos of footprints those which are the prints of truth. To the open mind it would appear that the inner meaning of incarnation is an aspect of such truth.

Today, when the attainments of science have revealed to us that we are not a special creation but bear in our very structure the insignia of those basic elements common to all creation, the very idea of incarnation is thereby widened and deepened. It can embrace the discovery of God in the world as a presence whose flashing into recognition may be uncovered anywhere and at any time. If we consider the basic Christian vision in relation to the still living tragedies of ancient Greek literature, we shall see not only the greatness of the change, but its impressive power. The dramas of ancient Greece celebrated the implacability of fate and the heroic assertion of the human will despite its irredeemable situation. What Christianity celebrates is the reversal of this order. The capitulation exacted by the gods is no longer arbitrary, for the god himself enters the suffering of the human world. By his presence within it he illuminates and redeems the human soul. The recognition of Christianity has been of the strength of vulnerability – a revolution in thought. (But this revolution has links that carry it backward as well as forward – to those formulations of myth and story which long preceded the Greek experience, and which are not peculiarly Western.)

The descent of divinity into the figure of Jesus and its cataclysmic outcome is an inevitable tragedy to which Judas is as necessary as Christ. It accents the barely supportable nature of the divine-human encounter – as

4

though humanity is blinded by the power of the infinite light, so that light and darkness are engaged in a perpetual battle without which there could be no transformation. For the ultimate reconciliation is found in heaven.

This is an inward drama. Of this drama, the drama of Jesus as the Christ, we are the inheritors. For almost 2,000 years it has been the focus for the spiritual journey of Western man. Now, the truth that it holds is opening out as a flower opens, from an apparently irresistible necessity. As it moves within, the external drama is suffering a metamorphosis, and the creature struggling to be born will bear a different shape. What this shape will be we do not yet know, since the horizons of our understanding are extending already towards a wider interpretation of the whole cosmos and ourselves within it. Though still opposed by some, this wider interpretation is also emerging from within science itself in terms which raise echoes within the mystical experience of centuries. This circular movement may be profoundly creative – but we are only at its beginning.

For the Western world the idea of incarnation has been embodied in a single focus, Jesus as the Christ. This still powerful myth is not diminished because today we have before us the possibility of moving beyond this single focus. Now, we are able to realise consciously that a single focus holds within it the greater whole – as the hologram holds the reflection of the whole within the part. Here again, scientific discovery, that of the hologram, endorses the age-old insights of mysticism, of poetry, of vision. 'To see a world in a grain of sand . . . . and eternity in an hour.'[1]

So that this focus in a point of time – the identification of incarnation with Jesus – has also been seen as a dynamic action which is out of time, and not only in the theological doctrine of his pre-existence, for by implication the whole of humanity is included in him. Incarnated, the transcendent becomes the immanent. Again, this vision, on the whole esoteric within the church, is not peculiar to Christianity. The Buddhist too can say: 'Look within; thou art Buddha.'

The incarnate Christ overshadows the historical Jesus who can be seen as prophet and as archetypal figure with resemblances in many cultures. He is a figure charged with ambiguities, and because of that with manifold meaning. The widespread rejection of the special divinity of Jesus in this century reflects the failure of the church, certainly. But it reflects also the stance of Judas who could not bear the light of the divine countenance but covered it in darkness; so, in parallel, within our darkened world the denial of the spirit is bringing us to the edge of destruction. Where God is crucified, the veil of the temple is rent. Once more, in the language of imagery we find truth sheltered.

[1] William Blake: *Auguries of Innocence*, poetical work of William Blake. O.U.P., 1928.

Jesus as the Christ has been the source of impassioned devotion down the centuries – sometimes for good, sometimes for evil – and no changes in thought can invalidate what that means. Its meaning will survive the decline of institutions, and the expansion of our horizons beyond the Christian era. For it is the experience of the Christian era which itself has made possible a changing future. The development of human thought moves in a spiral in which we turn upon the past in order to ascend at all. To forget this is to cut off the roots that nourish us.

Epiphany, the manifestation of God, can only be realised where the divine-human encounter takes place under conditions where the divine assumes the 'bounded' nature of the world.[1] It is the flash of this encounter which reveals the fire of the spirit.

Here, too, we move into the language of imagery, which (with that also of music) is the only language in which our sense of what is ineffable in our experience can, so far, be expressed.

If today, we do not return to a recognition of the significance of these things we are in danger of an atrophy of those faculties by which the fullness of human life is experienced. This fullness is not the impossible autonomy of mankind, but its awareness of its place in that harmony of creation whose mysterious summons to the human spirit has been called the sense of God. In the contemporary world, if science itself is moving towards those frontiers where rational analysis dissolves and the barely expressible is reached, then we may be seeing the first tentative approaches towards one another of the insights of religion and those of science. Indeed, this process appears already to be beginning.

The spider weaves out of itself its web – that externalisation of its being which maintains its existence. So do we. But the web is finite and transitory. It is the process which endures. Out of the mysterious impetus within the mind the human being creates the convoluted structures by which it lives, without which it would have no sustenance, would languish and die. In primitive societies food for the body is seen as a part of this procedure, by which invocation – blind and silent within the spider, vocal and symbolic within humanity – effects the achievement of the hunt. In sophisticated man the remnants of this magical routine still exist where a ceremony of grace is performed before meals. (Incorporated with an added significance in the familiar words, Take, eat, this is my body.)

In the Christian church the doctrine of incarnation has been offered as a crystallisation of that basic process by which humanity summons towards itself what is beyond itself, and yet inseparably a part of its very life. We carry in our blood and bones this inescapable imperative. The shape that we

[1] The word 'bounded' is borrowed from George Steiner's *Antigones* in quite another context.

6

give to it in order that we may be able at once to bear its assault and to make it visible – thus easing our acknowledgement of it – has most often been called religion.

But for developed man religion is not the only form in which this dynamic imperative is housed. For many, it is housed as imperiously in art – an art which has so often used the manifestations of religion as its framework, so that the two aspects have achieved a kind of marriage. It has been housed also in the sometimes ecstatic journey of the mystic. It informs and fills the movement of love and compassion. It belongs to the very being of language, to the fulfilment of sexuality, to politics, to philosophy, and now, perhaps, at last, it is to be acknowledged in the explorations of science. Awareness of its widespread meaning is stirring in our contemporary community at the very moment of acute danger – a moment of danger in which the spider in its hole is as threatened as humanity itself, because in the disintegration, the fragmentation, the externalisation of our life we have forgotten the basic pieties, not only of our own existence, but of all existence.

To ride on this newly cleansing tide without drowning we need the strength of powerful conviction. We need to recognise anew the wisdom of a saying that survives from more than 400 years before the birth of Christ, that 'visible existences are a sight of the unseen'.[1]

Uttered long before the advent of Christendom, this phrase is an expression of the experience of incarnation as the basis of all life. Suborned by the narrowed channelling of the Christian faith, Western mankind forgot the larger implications, and in doing so cast off a great part of its birthright. We are living in the era either of the correction of this imbalance, or else of the death of our civilisation – and perhaps of our earth.

'The encounter with the transcendent' says Roger Garaudy, 'is the commonest, the most specific human experience, the experience of creation.'[2] Set in a context inimical to religious vision, this remark expresses none the less the validity of the experience of a dimension in human being which is at once within and beyond itself. It acknowledges the profound and central importance of the fact that access to what is beyond us is drawn out from within us and nourishes our life. To that degree, though in terms other than those of incarnational imagery, Karl Marx himself was aware that the era of the division of nature and spirit was over, that if we are to go further this opposition must be itself transcended.

Thus the statement of Anaxagoras, quoted above, remains prophetic of our own day and its possibility of extended insights. Looked at in the light of the enormous needs of our time it acquires overtones that may carry us

[1] Anaxagoras of Clazomenae (fragments only survive of his book on nature).
[2] Roger Garaudy: *Marxism in the 20th Century*, transl. René Hague. Collins, 1970.

beyond the dualistic thinking of the man who uttered it. On the borderline of earlier changes in Greek thought, Anaxagoras recalls to us those who preceded him.

If our perspective on incarnation has narrowed since the advent of Christianity, we have only to look backward beyond the Socratic era to see in the earlier thought of ancient Greece horizons of incredible reach. For the pre-Socratic Greeks the Logos was itself expressed in the immediacy of being. Vision and thought were not divided. When that division came, largely with Aristotle, we in the West took the first steps towards that fragmentation of the world which has brought our contemporary community to the very edge of disaster. Today, in a world no longer seen as charged with the divine, dedication slackens and vision dies.

But the cycles of life and understanding are moved by currents inaccessible, in the end, to our manipulation. The pendulum is beginning its alternating swing. A life geared to the external, the calculable, the manipulable, to the rational, divorced from its roots in the supra-rational, is beginning to display its barrenness and the accumulation of its evils is becoming intolerable. The illusion of inexhaustible power is cracking. We are beginning to see that the limits to human autonomy are set, not by our own will, but by the nature of life itself – that it is existence itself which presents us not only with moral imperatives but with the necessity of proceeding in harmony with the movement of the universe as a whole. At every moment of history audible to the poet and the mystic, the chords of this harmony are becoming audible also to the tentative explorations of those scientists who are themselves reaching the limit of the measurable, suspecting the dissolution of all things into an all-permeating and invisible creative energy.

This immeasurable perspective is new, not in itself, but in what is becoming the historical possibility of its conscious formulation in terms that are not overtly religious.

The conviction of a hidden significance in existence has always been present to the human imagination as the motive force of a continually recurring and *corresponding* vision within all cultures and all civilisations, whatever the superficial differences and the jealousy with which they have been guarded. This vision has been mediated by the sacred figure, the object of worship, in which its power has been momentarily arrested and made visible.

For Christianity this process has been centred on the figure of Jesus Christ as the only incarnation of the divine. The mistake of official Christianity appears to have lain both in its insistence on the historical uniqueness and finality of this role, and also in the suppression of its universal source. This narrowing, the imprisoning as it were of Jesus Christ within the limiting structures of church authority and exoteric presentation, has eroded recognition of his wider significance.

Today, for all but those pockets of fundamentalism which fight a rearguard action against the imminence of change, what has Jesus become? A figure walking in Galilee, his back towards us, as he passes into remote distances. He has become also that Other who walks beside us, and at the same time outdistances us, becoming beyond our straining gaze a mere speck in the distance. But the miracle remains that however far he goes – into what endless distances – we can never lose him. For those distances are within us. They belong to that infinity in whose encompassment the actuality of our transient personal being takes on its outline. Without the realisation of this encompassment the continuous separation of the minute particulars of every separate being could not take shape at all. This kind of dichotomy is in every direction the instrument of our perceptions, and of all that we make of them.

In the paradox also of our dual rootedness, in earth and in heaven, the figure of Jesus Christ becomes ourselves. For the truths that lie within Christianity are greater than its errors – and vastly more far-reaching. To lose sight of this is to lose a heritage.

For the movement of human life is always towards disclosure. The conception of incarnation is a part of that movement. When what is disclosed stands forth before us, it is recognised – and this is an ancient realisation. Disclosure, in the sense in which it has always been known, both to the poet and to a certain kind of philosopher, opens to us the flow of the universal with which the world of our differentiated experience is in tension. This knowledge has come down to us from as far back as the pre-Socratic Greeks, and, no doubt, in other forms, from much further.

What we are is realised in the flesh, whose ambiguities accent for us the metaphysical reality of our existence. How should the form exist without the god who inhabits it? Is not our very being exemplified in that breath whose other name is spirit? These are unfashionable ideas in a contemporary civilisation which has sought in all directions to emphasise the external and the calculable, as though they could exist alone. Human existence *is* transcendence, and transcendence demands incarnation.

None the less, our contemporary Western community has almost completely rejected such terms as incarnation, redemption, grace. In surviving pockets of religious allegiance these terms may still be used, but awareness of their meaning has dimmed. Outside these diminishing areas what such terms stand for appears altogether forgotten or dismissed. They are seen as superfluous to a life that is full of movement, acquisitions, noise, and superficiality. A widespread vulgarisation of taste has followed, a contempt of quality in favour of an all-pervading brashness, greed, and self-preoccupation. Or so it seems if one looks at the surface of the modern city life and its apparent retreat from both aesthetic and moral values – a condition echoed more often than not on the television screen, in the newspapers, in books published solely for a quick monetary profit, in 'popular' film and and theatre. The god of a commercial prosperity, a ceaseless flow of superfluous goods and their adjunct the advertising industry, exacts a tribute of time, energy, and raw material for a common consumption on a scale never seen before. Against this apparently unheeding background there rises the grim spectacle not only of the deployment of nuclear (and chemical) weapons, of endemic war, terror and starvation in many corners of the world, of the deadly irresponsibility of the pursuit of nuclear power, of unemployment and homelessness in the so-called prosperous countries, of an earth ravaged for the greed of men, of whole peoples deprived of their homelands and the integrity of their lives broken up.

Evil, exploitation, greed. These are not conditions newly sprung to life in our times. They have existed always – outside Eden. But their scale today is seen to be vast, their multiplication invades us everywhere. The sterility of their impact threatens not only the very foundations of our lives, but also the very life itself of the planet we have systematically violated.

Slowly, awareness of the sheer unviability of this situation is widening – in pockets of rebellion, in initiatives taken for a new mode of life, a new concept of economics, of politics, a vision of a society geared to those inward and profound motions of the soul which have been the jewel at the heart of the great world religions, however tarnished by power, compromise, corruption, and fanaticism.

There is no shortage of fanaticisms today – perhaps the last writhings of an animal that is threatened by inevitable destruction in the movement of time and history, if the final disaster does not overtake us. But where the West itself still has some of its essential freedoms, enclaves of new thought, blueprints for new structures of society are emerging, gatherings of people whose protests widen as slowly and as inevitably as the widening circles that follow the throwing of a single stone on to the surface of a pond.

What motivates such people? Perhaps, out of a forgotten ancestral wisdom an unformulated memory of the god, who, though slain in the winter of the heart, rises against the darkness of death and offers us a promise. The promise is felt – in the blood, in the undestroyed spirit, in that affirmation of life which carries the seed of the future and scatters it against all denial that it will find fertile ground. It will. It will because at the moment of greatest need once more the god descends, becomes incarnated. Known or unknown, he is present in the soul, and where the impact of his presence becomes imperative it does not matter whether he is openly confessed or not. One thing is sure. He is unlikely to be confessed in the old terms.

10

The language of imagery and symbol, largely and so sadly forgotten, falls strangely now on those who have evaded its power. But, in the end, it is perhaps the only language which can save us, for it holds meaning as a cup holds water – only it is never empty for its source is continually replenished in the very motion of our life. Though our community continually betrays such knowledge, by constricting its activity to explanation and analysis as though this is all 'the word' contains, language itself is an aspect of incarnation. Of that more, later on.

The themes of institutionalised religion are staled for the majority, and a revival of the sense of the spiritual is occurring most vitally outside the churches. It is the *source* of spirituality which is sought, and not the imperfect vehicles which have compromised its actuality for so long. Apart from defensive pockets of fundamentalism in retreat from the challenge of the future, the spiritual adventure is being undertaken more and more outside the authority, the hierarchy, and the sexism of most traditional religious bodies. Yet, acknowledged more and more from within, these stresses are also shaking the churches themselves.

Though in this context there may be reservations about the nature of the statistical methods, the work of the Alister Hardy Research Centre in Oxford has shown us that there is widespread an awareness among men and women of a dimension of their experience that is at once ineffable and unmistakable – for which they have no referent except a realisation of the penetration of the universe of sensory responses by what seems a transcendent and liberating power.

Notably, perhaps for the first time ever in our history, there occurred fairly recently in the manifesto of a political party a direct reference to the spiritual dimension in human living.[1]

Each of these happenings is, in its own way, an affirmation of the reality of incarnation, whether the name is there or not. They take their place with the possibilities also of that new relationship between religion and science which appears already to be coming about, though here, so far, all is speculation, and tentative.

For the most part disregarded, unelucidated by the majority of people, these occurrences are pointers towards the possibility of regeneration. The advancing awareness of Western humanity has apparently reached a watershed where those who go before to prepare the way have sighted horizons that are new to the general consciousness but not new to those powers of the spirit which have shaped them in image and symbol and ceremony through many centuries. The formerly esoteric is becoming, gradually, exoteric. We are awakening not only from 'Newton's sleep'[2] but

[1] The Ecology Party, 1983 (later The Green Party).
[2] William Blake.

11

also from that long blindness where the meaning of incarnation has been obscured by the worship of the abstract and the external – as though these had an existence *sui generis* without reference to those forces of life which at once affirm and feed all living things. For that which is incarnated is at once the root and the crown of the tree of life.

CHAPTER II

The Disturbed Balance

By what right, it might be asked, do we assume a validity in the conception of incarnation, since it presupposes an attitude to knowledge beyond the processes of logic, and beyond the assumption of rationality as *the* supreme value? We might point out that the apparently limitless explorations of human ingenuity in its experience of the reasoned activities of calculation and the technology that is dependent on calculation has achieved a kind of giantism that is hollow. Within these articulated but lifeless structures achieved by abstraction the human soul rattles like a single pea in an emptied and withered pod – directionless, imprisoned, in the end perhaps frantic to get out. For the pod itself is shrivelled and diminished by the compulsive activities which are going on outside it and seem more powerful than itself. The 'whither' and the 'why' appear to have disappeared from the general context of human existence in the addictive excitements of a dizzying 'how'. Motion for its own sake has taken over and has all the attributes of a meaningless whirligig.

We might also turn for an answer to the story of human history as it unfolds before us today, presenting us with horizons of anthropological knowledge undreamed of two generations ago. Looking backward in history we see the maintaining of the advancement of the human world as dependent always on the felt presence of what is beyond the world. The framework of this paradox has been the necessary context of self-realisation. We might point out the brevity, in time, of the industrial revolution and the technological revolution which has succeeded it, and whose defiance of metaphysics is now being seen as an empty cry. We might point out the accumulating and apparently endemic nature of a type of poverty in the world which is relatively new, and which is the product of a world order that is without direction and without accountability beyond superficial and selective material gain which bears no relation to need.

There is nothing new in cruelty and indifference; but there is a certain newness in the results of the domination of financial manoeuvres which bring excess of prosperity worldwide, for a few, and a novel crucifying type of indigence for many. These many are a new class of people – the totally

13

dispossessed. (Here, the incarnation of the god is mocked, and the god himself destroyed.)

In all these things the limits of rationalised processes conducted for their own sake and without inner direction stare us in the face, just as they confront us also with the spuriousness of 'success', and of that 'efficiency' which leaves out of account those attitudes of the mind and the heart to which efficiency is marginal, or simply not relevant.

Operating in isolation reason is a castrated organ. It is only fully active when it is attendant on those human powers which have been called the powers of the spirit. Reason may appear the glory of man, since its development in us has reached heights inaccessible to any other species. But it is not fulfilled unless it is illumined from that Source of our existence which we share with every living creature – as we share also, though more consciously, profound instinctual responses to the fact of *being in the world*. These responses are a part of the impact of life in its immediacy, in its actuality, and they present us with laws of precedence which we neglect at our peril. To these responses the great metaphors of the religious world belong. (Theologies are an altogether subsequent structure.)

Exactly how far the possession of reason does differentiate us from the animals may be more in question in these days than formerly – since a closer knowledge of animal life has accented its potential resemblance to ourselves. Consequently, in response to the new tide of awareness already emphasised, there is coming into being a rising concern for all the living creatures of the earth, and an evocation of horror at the de-naturing of the life of those animals which provide large sections of mankind with food, and whom we had begun to treat not as sentient creatures but as things. Many of us are coming to understand the wisdom of the so-called 'primitive' whose respect for the animals he hunted was total, and with whom he felt a magical and symbiotic relationship. When we consider that the powers of science have also brought us to genetic engineering, the split in contemporary consciousness becomes even more evident – and questions of the integrity of knowledge itself rise up before us. These are moral issues of profound relevance to the future of mankind, and to the threat of the self-destruction of our own humanity. Does the power to clone, for instance, confer on us the necessity to clone? – or is there an enduring meaning in the conception of blasphemy? In these directions too the meaning of incarnation becomes suddenly apposite.

What *is* a living creature?

Despite its occasional direction towards despair, the philosophy of existentialism has taught us something of an answer to this question. At least, it has brought us back, with sharpness, to the immediacies of experience, and away from the closed circles of abstraction.

14

Merleau-Ponty has pointed out that our existence realises itself in the body, that the body and its existence presuppose each other, and that therefore existence is what he calls 'a perpetual incarnation'.[1]

The body's responses are acute and manifold. The manipulative mind may analyse and direct them – but the knife that dissects destroys the living creature. When we pick up a dead bird from the ground where has its life gone? What was its life? Dissolved on the air, the pulse of its song, its sweetness, has passed for the hearer into some channel of memory where its imprisonment in time and the occasion is transcended. The body of the bird is dead, but that which informed its body still exists on the receiving air and is never lost. It exists also in the consciousness of those who were aware of it. It has become a part of us – and the mystery of memory is not yet solved by an analysis of the pathways of the brain, and may never be so solved.

Our experience of the bird and our experience of ourselves are indissolubly united. The song, we are told, affirms a territory, but this explanation does not define, does not remotely touch, its sweetness, or that hearing it may have changed our lives. The feathers of the dead body are not essentially pitiful, for they have conveyed for a moment of time that vibration of divinity which belongs to the timeless. And what is divinity? At once the goal and the summons that has haunted the human race?

The bypassing of the sense of incarnation, its relegation to the outmoded procedures of a religion supposed to be out of touch with contemporary imperatives has clouded the understanding of the West. Not to see the world as impregnated with what is beyond the world, not to recognise behind and beyond those perceptions of the senses which permeate our lives that other dimension of being which alone gives form to the world of time is to live without direction – as though, travelling the vast ocean of existence we were to deny the necessity of paying any attention to that guiding Pole whose constant light has given us our principles of navigation.

That Pole itself is an indicator that existence in time is only *realisable in awareness* against the backcloth of the timeless – God being, in the phrase of the 15th-century Nicholas of Cusa, the 'coincidence of opposites', so that the movement of the human mind's attainment of consciousness is dialectical. For the darkened sea of our existence itself evokes the guiding Pole that shines in the supernal heavens. Or, so it seems – and this is merely the interaction of the human and the divine pictured in another dimension of the mind. To speak of these things at all is to speak of necessity in metaphor and image.

In terms of human existence as a whole, the *hubris* of contemporary Western man has been very shortlived. Now, as it threatens to bring on

[1] Merleau-Ponty: *Phenomenology of Perception*, Part I, chap. 5, transl. Colin Smith. Routledge & Kegan Paul, 1962.

itself its own nemesis, its arrogance is halted by a deep and growing uneasiness. Something more than a mere remembrance of the past has entered the contemporary consciousness – as awareness that the past, which we had thought discardable, is present *with us,* and insistently. What is beginning to move within us is not merely a recurrence of forgotten pieties, nor only a sense of deprivation. Something has shifted in the atmosphere of the times, a growing, inescapable recognition that in the turns of thought on the spiral of our existence we are suddenly aware of the living presence in a new form of what has gone before. Our newest perceptions today hold before us as in a mirror image the divinations that have preceded us – as it were clouded and half concealed in as yet heretical scientific suggestions, in the uneasy self-examination of institutionalised religion, in post-existential, and above all post-positivistic philosophy, and even in the latest searchings of the pseudo-science of psychology which are known as psycho-synthesis.

In this incipient revolution humility is called for. Like blasphemy, like redemption, like incarnation itself, humility is a word long cast out.

If the meaning of incarnation does indeed creep back into the vocabulary of Western man, it will be not in a single focus, as before, but in an expanding, a travelling illumination going before us as a pillar of fire in the night of our redeemed journeying out of the darkness of self-destruction.

Writing in 1934, the French philosopher Alain remarked: 'The errors of religion are far less dangerous for religion than for those who criticise it without looking at its principles.'[1] The truth of this observation strikes at the heart of our contemporary blind rejections which have shrugged off the perennially relevant along with the essentially outgrown.

Our community has been living out of a great inner emptiness, in which its achievements, despite their remarkable quality, have had no true foundations. But, fated to return in any still living community, the gods are indestructible. Their return will be staged in new but recognisable forms – that is, recognisable to those who have understood the meaning that the imagery of the gods has held. For the old forms exist not only in the long memory of our race, in our blood and bones, but in the timeless archetypes on which the perilous scaffolding of our for ever destroyed and renewed edifices of hope are raised.

Our civilisation is at this moment profoundly shaken. Its apparent but illusory confidence skates on the surface of deep and possibly engulfing waters whose existence it tries to deny or evade. The philosopher Alain also said that 'the disturbances of the knowing subject must finally take their place among positive truths'.[2] Our disturbances are surfacing, but whatever

---

[1] Alain: *The Gods* (1934), chap 8, transl. Richard Pevear. Chatto and Windus, 1973.
[2] *Ibid*: Introduction.

epiphany the consequent evocation of the god reveals, it will not simply repeat what went before.

In fact, if the acknowledgement of disturbance faces us with truth, then this is advancement – for that disquiet is not faced is one of the destructive expressions which present us with a lightless world. The pretence that our world society is not sick, that the very basis of its economics, its politics, and its religious intransigencies do not need to be challenged contributes to the oncoming of a crisis in which the whole planet may go down. The process of recovery involves the confrontation of the barrenness of a form of living in which the reality of the spirit is not simply denied, but perverted. This condition at the very roots of our collective living is visibly before us, and is itself a denial of incarnation. A widened recognition of the deep meaning in the idea of incarnation will be a part of the process of change whether it is so named or not.

At least, if the mounting sense of disturbance brings us back to face our rejections it will be to face them nakedly, without defence. The concept of repentance, of *metanoia,* is alien to the contemporary attitude. In a culture of incessant noise and incessant movement what can be heard of the still small voice, or indeed of the healing power of stillness itself? Yet, very slowly, an awareness of the truth of such ideas is re-entering the general consciousness. It is the first step towards regeneration.

The hitherto contemporary deafness to such words, outside the diminishing religious organisations – redemption, incarnation, grace, humility, repentance – has blinded us to the fact that their significance belongs intrinsically to the movement of the human heart. They are an expression of the inescapable centres at which the human aspiration towards the divine is both illumined and chastened. It is often said that the needs of contemporary mankind, in order to be met, demand a new vocabulary. But do they? If we are deaf to certain expressions of the human condition it is not because virtue has gone out of the expressions, but out of us. Such words have been a part of the vocabulary of Christendom for centuries, precisely because they spelt out the truths that emerged out of disturbance. Their equivalent will be found to exist elsewhere, wherever the organisations of other religions have not totally betrayed their original vision. Such words belong to the human condition because they reflect the nature of our existence, which is always summoned beyond its own failures.

Intrinsic to this summons is the sense of the visible world as the vessel of the invisible, of the flesh as lending form to the spirit, of incarnation as an endless process. The opening of new horizons of human knowledge of itself has been so rapid over less than two centuries, and so centred on the physical structures of the world, that it has induced the delusion that structure is all. If the exposed and the analysed were all, if they had no counterpart in the invisible, how should we discern them? The dichotomy of opposites is inescapable as the foundation on which the very conceivability of existence is established.

We have forgotten the imperative need for a blessing on the work we do, and that all true work is done to the glory of God. Once more, so-called outmoded language bears a message that we neglect at our peril.

Why is it that the exhibition of giant robots with limbs and bodies articulated in imitation of the anatomical structure of insects fills us with dismay? To see on the screen one of these inventions lurching across a rural landscape is to witness what seems an enormous caricature or a progenitor of nightmare. In these machines what seems evidenced is a human ingenuity which has no anchorage in the sensibilities of perception, but has produced a kind of non-being of a size and type which threatens domination.

A peregrinating machinery on such a scale is not only a caricature of an anatomy from which its planning has been derived. It trespasses also on the meaning of the phrase *laborare est orare,* by which work is honoured as a kind of reciprocity between effort and significance.

To say that the landscape is insulted by the progress across it of such a monstrosity may well be called emotive. But if feeling has no place in the relation between mankind and the work it lives by, both it and the work will eventually wither together. Look at the exposed wastes of monoculture, the life-denying practices of soil erosion, or the wastelands of enormous cities, and we see that a balance is distorted by a worship of both largeness and spendthrift use. Nature conserves, and she conserves in a harmony and a mutually benefiting exchange of activity.

Does this mean that our manipulations of certain kinds of knowledge are more than inexpedient, are forbidden? Perhaps – and the Faustian scene may have a terrible reality, and not only on the nuclear question.

Freedom is real only when it works within a willing assent to the innate imperatives which are the foundation of all life, and are reciprocal. This is discoverable within the pages of the Bible, as it is discoverable also within the uncontaminated soul wherever it is found. An uncontrolled technology threatens us with dehumanisation. There is no excess that does not bring its own nemesis, and unbridled invention may bring a devastating recoil on those who invent without reference to the rhythms of natural exchange between man and environment.

A crisis in awareness, a crisis in relationship has brought about the destruction of forests, of animal habitat, of our own acknowledgement of the imperatives we have traditionally obeyed and which were conveyed to us by our instinctual responses to that which surrounds us and of which we are an inseparable part. The rhythms of nature move also within us, and when these rhythms are destroyed our sense of a direction to what we are about diminishes. A destroyed orientation has focused us on ourselves, so that all that we handle is seen as designed for our own gratification.

Here, nothing is realised as the vehicle of incarnation. Everything is contained in the exposure of its detail, its laid-bare anatomy, its analysed chemistry, its interacting neurons. It is from this reductionism that we are beginning to emerge. We are escaping into regions of the mind where the awareness of incarnation is no longer enclosed only within the rituals of a particular religion whose institutions are perhaps themselves becoming increasingly questionable. Such a reopening of the doors of perception will confront us with ancient insights at another level, and is perhaps our only means of redemption.

Recurrence, alternation, death and renewal, response to the internal biorhythms which move us are a part of our endowment and our perennial experience. These occurrences are in tune with the earth's breathing, the movement of the stars, and the inseparability from our consciousness of the movement of time.

That the sense of the eternal is a product of the realisation of time would seem to be evident. It is not simply that the pathos of the transient has no meaning except against the obduracy of the enduring, but that the enduring itself melts into the different obduracy of durations acknowledged by the mind as beyond its power to assimilate, but not to envisage. The human conceptions of vastness and illimitability become fantastic structures in regions where time loses its recognisable sequences and time and space interpenetrate each other. Astronomical figures outspin realisation both in the macrocosmic and the microcosmic world, and the universe becomes a dizzying dance. Against these half envisaged marvels, our grasp on the movement of time slips and founders. Yet, daily we experience both its tyranny and moments when, miraculously, it ceases – and we say that 'time stood still'.

The star over Bethlehem manifests this phenomenon, at the point of entry of the divine, the eternal, into the human and the timebound. The inner meaning of the story of the birth of Christ illuminates with an absolute simplicity the mutuality of time and the timeless which is hidden in the dizzying calculations of the astronomers. Both have their origins within the human mind. Who shall say that the one holds truth and not the other?

Legend fabricates the material of reality. Within the interstices of time it inserts those truths which are beyond time. Nothing is proven. But the authentic registers its presence and is recognised. It is not the fault of legend that today many wear blinkers.

All we know of time is that it is inseparable from, perhaps emerges from, our consciousness, and a sense of its flux is perhaps an illusion of our own transience. Every moment of our conscious experience reshapes both what has gone before and what is expected. In what is expected, in our half-shaped intentionalities, we discern beyond our own will an unformed expectation that for ever lures us on. This, too, is perhaps a warning of the always imminent descent of the god, the inescapable encounter with incarnation.

Beneath our visible preoccupations the currents of our unacknowledged and deeper life carry those eddies which do not interrupt our passage between life and death, but sustain it. Like the whirlpool itself these eddies form spirals of meaning whose shapes and patterns are a part of the endless repetitions which unite all things in the gyrations of the cosmic dance of which we are a part. Not strange to the Eastern mind, such realisations are entering the streams of thought of Western mankind, at points where they may prove as effective as the points sought by acupuncture are to the physical body.

It is in time that we make visible what is hidden. It is in time that we see incarnated that which has waited on the threshold of our perception, and which we have called the eternal. Without time, and the spatiality with which it is indissolubly united, we could neither evoke nor recognise the Other, that which is beyond ourselves, which encompasses us, and whose encompassment creates us – God.

For the interaction of contraries is the pulse of life. It is here in these irresistible processes, that we encounter the inevitability of incarnation. To the shaken mind of contemporary Western humanity the eclipse of this perception is emerging as judgement. But the moment of rescue from this condition is stirring within its very extremity. It will bring with it an expansion of our understanding of the word incarnation itself beyond the literal meaning of 'made flesh'.

Judgement is a reality – and we are encountering it now.

The characteristic attitude of our times has been labelled that of 'anxiety', or of alienation. The deepening awareness of ourselves as 'thrown' into existence has had, for the majority, no antidote in a revealed and authoritative religion whose precepts formerly upheld the individual within a world view which however extreme its terms provided a definitive framework on which his or her life could be contained – or from which it could be outlawed.

For the outlaw, too, is the child of the Weltenschaung which he has rejected, and all that he does and is refers back to its inescapable presence. The pervasion of guilt is balanced by the inevitability of judgement, and defiance has an object by which it is recognisable. In the medieval world the church provided the security of these antinomies. Later, with the rise of Protestantism, they have been contained within power politics, 'patriotism', and the tyrannies of ruthless economic progress – and the other-worldly dimension has receded.

Today, the authority of the church, of any church, is deeply eroded. Even within Roman Catholicism this is beginning to be so despite increases in numbers in some parts of the world. The progress of the white-clad Pope among thousands of spectators as he has visited the faithful in several countries has seemed to many a curious anachronism whose relevance to the central problems of our times requires some more well-founded accenting than what is superficially sensational in his progress. The drama he presents has become for very many people a drama within a closed world – and our contemporary world is seen to be wide open.

The rise of individual awareness which accompanied Protestantism and was fostered by the spread of education set free unlimited energies which were as little to be checked as a rising tide. Industrialisation, the awakening political consciousness of the working-class, two world wars of an appalling destructiveness, the menace of Nazism and the horror of the holocaust – all these things shook the foundations of the Western community. But they were accompanied by opening scientific horizons never before imagined – one of these being the splitting of the atom – and by an also unparalleled technological achievement that has taken men to the moon, made possible the questionable processes of genetic engineering, and given us the power to destroy not only our own species but all species.

The external world and its possibilities of exploitation and manipulation has claimed the attention of the West almost totally, focusing concentration on the analytical faculties of the mind – a process fostered also by the rise of monolithic communism wherein modifications of Marx largely eliminated those aspects of his thought which had wider implications. Now, these things too are suffering a checking of pace.

Within recent years an explosion of energy has generated an excess of objects of consumption, of unlimited travel, of ever-accelerating speed, noise and movement – of a kind of drunkenness of activity wherein thought is held at bay, and the very conception of the significance of the inner life of mankind has been ignored.

Yet it is there. Inevitably, it is beginning to make itself felt. Formulated by existentialism, the condition of alienation has festered – is festering – for the most part underground. Repressed anxiety and uncertainty issues in violence, or in its antithesis which is apathy. Glaringly unequal economic conditions breed hopelessness and frustration. A society geared to 'the market' ruthlessly exploits circumstance at the cost of whoever is left behind. The meaning in life is lost in the continual endeavour to 'keep up'. To escape self-examination, everything is trivialised. Novelty is worshipped as a safe substitute for true change. Blindly, the greed for possession and power ravage the surface of the earth.

Yet underneath these stereotypes of attitude the palpitating variety of humanity endures. Little visible on the surfaces of life as yet, perceptions deepen and uneasiness lifts its head. Here and there, recognition of an extremity of danger, of accumulating disorder, surfaces and promises to become the catalyst of change. Impetus towards change is at first dispersed, barely visible, but it accumulates. From deep within its compulsions what is released is the dammed up force of that neglected inner life without which the human journey will run into the desert of sterility.

We are coming to realise perhaps that there is a point where Life itself takes charge. If we refuse to receive its signals, no doubt our civilisation will go down as others have gone down. Yet, this time, for the first time, ours is potentially a global civilisation, and we have dared to think it different. If our sapped confidence is curable, we have to learn that we too are not immune from answerability to God, that hidden within the deeper mind, within the heart, the kernel of what is human is itself the seed of divinity.

CHAPTER III

Forms of Divinity

LOOKING BACK OVER HISTORY WE CAN recognise today how the narrowed perspective of official Christianity has obscured the potential width of meaning in the idea of incarnation. This perspective has dismissed as irrelevant to the allegedly final and unique revelation in Jesus Christ those forms of divinity discoverable within all cultures. Today, we may see any question of 'finality' in terms other than those of Christian institutions – that is to say, in terms of inclusivity rather than exclusivity.

The projection of human needs and aspirations on to the various forms of divinity has accompanied the human journey whether in great civilisations or in obscure tribes. Now occurring for the first time in history, does the bringing together of the whole world signal the end of that process? If that is so, then Jesus Christ will indeed be the last bearer of incarnation in the form of the god, the last external redeemer figure.

This recognition of finality bears a different emphasis from that of the churches, since it places Christ as the peak of a long succession, and renders the scandal of particularity emptied of continuing relevance in the old terms. Nor is the sense of the Christ *within* us new. It has been present, paradoxically and confusedly, even within the emphasis on externality.

Movement towards clarification of this question appears to evoke disturbance and even shock in religious quarters. None the less, the coming into consciousness of what has formerly been projected contributes to the beginning of what may well be the new age of the spirit, equally foretold by Karl Marx, but in different terms.

To Marx, for antiquity the divine was enthroned in nature in the form of the visible heavens, and this was a closed world in which the spirit was imprisoned. Then came the age of the Son, the equally closed world that is Christianity, bounded by the incarnate Word and the written word of the Bible. The third age was to be for him the promise of the freeing of the spirit from the tyranny of the other worldly transcendence. The ultimate perfection of society was seen by him as a linear process, and his vision millenarian. For Marx, mind *emerged* from matter.

23

He asserted that 'all mythology subdues, controls, and fashions the forces of nature in the imagination and through the imagination; it disappears therefore when real control over these forces is established'.[1]

Setting aside arguments for this or that specific political or economic organisation, these words of Marx express the climate of the mind in which our community has been living, which in the end it is finding debilitating, disorienting, and destructive. The new age that hovers before us now is not appearing in Marx's terms at all. Today, both the lost world of antiquity and the era of Christianity reveal themselves as seed-beds of a future that is moving in a spiral, inevitably returning on itself, and the nature of existence is seen as at once both cyclic and ever-opening upon expanding vistas. Our operations upon nature are beginning to be seen as demanding from us responses to a transcendent, universal, and pre-existent harmony that informs the whole of our universe, and which we betray at our peril. In itself, Mind becomes immanent, not emergent, and incarnation therefore a felt aspect of truth.

If, today, we are seeing the conviction of the dawning of a new age surfacing in many directions, it carries with it the dangers of a too easy plausibility and an uncritical, acceptance of those excesses which do not understand the absolute relevance of the past to the present. In fact, recognition of the imminence of a new age fulfils a longstanding tradition which also, though differently from Marx, declared first the age of the Father, then the age of the Son, and after that the age of the Spirit. This is, in these modes of thought, the fulfilment of Pentecost. The return of this *kind* of thought in whatever terms it is expressed, necessitates a resurgence of aspects of the human mind which in the West have been in eclipse, not simply since Newton and Descartes, but – as has already been stated – preparedly, since Aristotle.

Such a movement towards the future would entail, and in fact has begun to entail, for the dominant Western 'rationality' as it faces change, a magnetic pull towards those Eastern attitudes which it has suppressed and denigrated within itself. (We have seen happening also a more blatant obverse in the taking over by Eastern countries of the technological expertise and the money-obsessed superficialities of the West.)

In the accomplishment of such exchanges it behoves us to discover in the attitudes of the past those kernels of perennial meaning which will seed a truly creative future. Without a conscious balance in the forces which are moving into change, without a renewed awareness of an ongoing significance in the idea of incarnation whatever the forms of its expression, and however it is named, we shall lose our way in the immense dangers of this moment of history when we hover on the edge of self-destruction.

[1] Marx: *A Contribution to the Critique of Political Economy*, p. 211. Progress Publishing, Moscow, 1970.

To attain the future we return upon the past, where the future is already present. In the heretics of church history we see already approaching today's moment – in the form of a challenge to the too-entrenched certainties of orthodoxy and the refusal of church authority as necessarily superior to a prophetic, inward, and inspired personal vision. It is to an awareness of the sources of this inward vision that we now need to turn.

Deep below the surfaces of the inductive method which has dominated the mental processes of our times there lies a movement of the human mind whose motion, like the motion of the sea, is the same everywhere. This is seen no less in antiquity, in those who preceded the emergence of an eventually self-dependent rationality, than in those whose approach has been entirely by way of symbolic forms. In his consideration of the nature of the soul, Aristotle himself expressed *dunameis* as power – a power in which 'interiority and exteriority are held in a peculiar unity in tension'.[1] Essentially, the source of such power is inward. Therefore the heart of its exercise is found, not in its expression, but in its own primal force. This force is, so to speak, incarnated in action, a manifestation of that which dwells within the human soul. To deny the existence of what has been called the soul is to deny what would seem to be the very foundation of all human activity, mental or physical – and the realisation that this is so becomes a necessity of continuing human existence itself, if it is to remain human.

To the original Greek idea of reason there was a religious ground – a realised depth of awareness which involved the sacral element in human response. The sense of this we have lost. To rediscover it will be a necessity of the future. An equal and related necessity will be the recognition that 'all knowledge is symbolic'.[2] Where this is understood the split between idealism and realism ceases to exist and the heart of hermeneutics is seen to be the communion of all things as aspects of one whole, and of one another. Are we living in a moment when this insight may be recoverable?

Such an attitude assumes a stance that is deeply, innately religious. It inescapably denotes that the essential nature of mankind and the motion of its being are one manifestation. The reductionism of conventional modern science with its rejection of the kind of ontology which preceded metaphysics itself, has destroyed the complete association of mankind with the inward impetus of all creation which was the core of the Logos philosophy. Of course there have been rebellions against such destructiveness, and such rebellions are now achieving their moment in the reaction of the pendulum swing of human thought towards a new realisation that the creative insights of the past are indispensable to the achievement of a living future.

[1] Hans-Georg Gadamer: *Truth and Method*. Sheed and Ward, 2nd edition, 1979.
[2] *Ibid*: Friedrich Schlegel, as quoted.

The pre-Socratic Greeks took for granted the unity of being and thought – *physis* and *logos*. For Greek thought as a whole the word, the Logos, was not a perfected mankind as it became for Christianity. It was the essence of all being.

Some of the attitudes of Heraclitus (around 500 BC) though accommodated within his emphasis on change, suggest the necessity for the splitting of the Logos in order for it to be realised as active within time – a law of its manifestation being the appearance of the eternal within the temporal. This apparent opposition results in the creation of harmony – the famous bow and lyre saying – 'harmony consists of opposing tension like that of the bow and the lyre'.[1] In the temporal is disclosed the divine. This too, though differing in expression, is a manifestation of incarnation which moves as on the turn of a spiral towards what is becoming differently but relatedly expressible today. For pre-Socratic thought Being itself is the Logos and *possesses* mankind.

It is within these dimensions of understanding that the contemporary human community might achieve its own redemption both from the kind of self-destruction epitomised in the insane creation and accumulation of nuclear weapons and that destruction of our essential humanity which an unregulated and obsessive pursuit of technology may well bring about.

For the earliest Greeks the Logos was *heard*. For Plato, as for many who succeeded him, the image at the centre of human understanding was the light – seeing. It is interesting in this connection that for George Fox, the 17th-century Quaker, we 'hear' the light. All these attitudes and expressions relate to the destiny of human beings seen as illumination and response. As maker, mankind receives the creativity of his making only by the assent and permission of the gods. Which is to say, that he is answerable – and he is answerable because his being and the world's being are indivisible. Are we about to return to this awareness also?

'As early as the Homeric epic (probably 9th century BC) the light represents salvation.'[2] It does so also in the Upanishads, the sacred Sanskrit literature dating over centuries from around 800 BC. 'Now the light which shines beyond the heavens . . . in the highest and most exalted worlds, that is indeed the same as the light within man.'[3] For in the Upanishads too we find an implication related at a deep level to the perennial yearning of humanity for the presence of God in the world. Speaking of the One, Brahman – 'For He indeed is the Self within the heart . . . He who is in the

[1] Freeman: *Ancilla to the Pre-Socratic Philosophers (Fragments)*, as quoted. Blackwell, 1962.
[2] Ernst Cassirer: *The Philosophy of Symbolic Forms*, Vol. 2, transl. Manheim. O.U.P.
[3] *Chandogya Upanishad III*, xiii.

fire down here, He who is in the heart within, and He who is the Sun up there . . . He indeed is One.'[1] Here too the divine is brought down as shining visibly within his creation, of which mankind is an integral part.

In the Bhagavad Gita we read of Krishna (the god descended): 'the foolish mock at Me, at my descending like a human being. They do not know My transcendent nature, My supreme dominion over all that be.'[2] Krishna is seen as appearing in many incarnations, and here incarnation is personified as in Jesus. But the Bhagavad Gita also says: 'When one sees Eternity in things that pass away and Infinity in finite things, then one has pure knowledge.'[3] – and this is not rational knowledge but that knowledge of 'the heart' which lies at the core of all religions, affirming the actuality of what is called the divine. It is not discoverable in scholarship, though scholarship may elucidate it, but is open to all, even the simplest.

All these expressions have a profound bearing on the conception of incarnation. At its roots the centring of incarnation on mankind is itself symbolical. Repeatedly, the 'cosmic man' is envisaged as that which holds together in one centre the plurality and diversity of creation. He is the channel of recognition by which the spiritual fundament of our existence is realised.

Is there not a relation here with the words of the 17th-century Quaker, Robert Barclay, who said: 'a divine, spiritual and supernatural light is in all men; from that supernatural light or seed is *vehiculum Dei:* how that God and Christ dwelleth in it and is never separated from it; also how that it is received and closed within the heart, Christ comes to be formed and brought forth.'[4] Here too is another form of the inseparability of the divine from its manifestation in humanity. The difference in historical time and place is only in the word supernatural against which we now put a question mark.

Within Sufism there is a doctrine of the Perfect Man, the microcosm of the infinite who preceded the creation of the world, and provided a mirror image by which God was able to perceive himself. In a different way from that of Buddhism this too may be seen as the devolving upon mankind of the responsibility for the *realisation* of existence in consciousness. It is a form of manifestation of divinity seen as an integral part of the destiny of humanity itself. Its mythological structure does not disguise its relevance to the audacities of contemporary explorations of that universe of which humanity is an indissoluble part.

[1] *Maitri Upanishad VII*, para 7.
[2] *Upanishad II*, text 14.
[3] *Upanishad XVIII*, 20.
[4] Robert Barclay: An Apology for the True Christian Divinity, 1676.

Also, among the precursors of the cosmic Christ is the Vedic Purusha (circa 900 BC), who was sacrificed to the gods and survived a dismemberment from which the parts of the universe were formed. This was a sacrifice at the beginning of time, and differs from the Christian story, but a basic resemblance exists in the notion of potent sacrifice, the power implicit in a miraculous survival of death, and in the centring on the figure of man. Essentially, this myth is a much earlier hypostatisation related to that of the Christian Trinity where the deity is seen as hypostatised in three Persons.

Theological attitudes like that of the Trinity represent summations of the truths of an experience prior to their selective formulation, and to the dangers of ossification which face them. The prior experience is intuitive and common to all peoples. To dismiss this dimension of human life as irrelevant to modern mankind, as though it was merely the product of the shortcomings of religious institutions, is the illusion of our century's *hubris*. The loss of the ability to think in imagery would be the loss of the very ground of the human mind.

We are only human in so far as we see our very existence as a dialectical process. Without that which is beyond us – the setting in which we become visible to ourselves – how should we be defined? That which defines us we call God but it is of itself indefinable and ineffable. This is a necessity not of logic but of Being, and humanity appears only viable *as* humanity in the shadow of this knowledge which of its nature, cannot be expressed directly but only in the living image, whose variable and paradoxical forms contain and display the dynamism of existence.

The expansion of the meaning of incarnation is of vital importance to the survival of mankind, and to the possibility of the opening out of the consciousness of humanity towards new horizons. If, for the West, the Christian era has been a necessary stage in the progress of self-realisation, which may well be, it is imperative that we recognise its central truths as illuminations, as pointers, to those new directions which will be the means of our shared regeneration as a species. As a part of this process the sense of divinity as revealed to us no longer in the projection of an outward focus but within ourselves is no new thought. It has accompanied the progress of the church throughout the Christian centuries as a half hidden but irresistible underground stream.

In their bitterness and disillusion with the church, or their total disregard of it, those in the West who have turned with a hasty and uncritical enthusiasm to the practices of Buddhism and Hinduism seem on the whole not to have understood either the historical role of Christianity or the meeting points of vision and illumination which are shared by all religions. Beyond and within the layers of ceremony and ritual whose strangeness may fascinate by its novelty there lies an inner experience which echoes and re-echoes across the world and history, and which moves as surely below the visible layers of Christianity as elsewhere. This kernel of truth, this light of the divine reflected in the human consciousness, is the same everywhere. That it is indestructible is the conviction of faith. It is only the forms in which we shape it which change.

Let us go back to the redeemer god, exemplified in many other directions as in Krishna, and, obliquely, in the creation story of the Purusha.

For the pre-Christian gnostics he who descends from heaven to redeem mankind is Man himself. Whether he takes form as a holy man or as a divine king, he is an image of God. Sometimes he is seen as the Saviour of the fallen virgin, who is also the Soul, or Wisdom, or stands under the ancient and traditional image of the 'Pearl'. It has been argued that these images had some influence on the ideas of St Paul.

It is also in many of the pagan gods that we see a powerful imagery of the permeation of the world by divinity, and also the inevitably interrelated action of life, death, and resurrection – the ritual of salvation. The story of Dionysos (who is also Bacchus, Zagreus, Adonis, Attis, and Tammuz) enacts the myth of the slain and resurrected god, long pre-dating the crucifixion of Christ. Eventually, in developed forms of society, the rites which were connected with the life-preserving rhythms of nature were internalised, becoming focused on the journey of the soul. The roots of the Christian interpretation of life lie deep, and are watered by strange and largely unacknowledged currents.

These currents form an ever-flowing, widening stream whose destination may be a remote and unimaginable ocean beyond our present conception. If we do indeed live in a moment of great change, we are borne on tides whose first springs lie in the remotest epochs of human history. In this process we have lost for a time the original Mother Goddess (except in the pale form of the Virgin Mary) and this is not without significance for the unbalanced culture of the contemporary Western world with its dominant and eventually destructive reliance on aggression, competition, and the analytical faculties of the mind divorced from their roots in the intuitive, the caring, the imaginative.

In Mādhyamika Buddhism, for instance, we find that both God and man are forms of the Absolute, of which they are individuations. There may be unlimited phenomenalisations (appearances) of the Buddha, and all beings may be considered as manifestations of God. These forms of expression arise for the Buddhist not within the boundaries of reasoned thought but, epistemically, beyond such thought, in the very ground of all true knowledge, Prajñā (which may be loosely translated as intuition). Forms of knowledge other than that originating with Prajñā are subsidiary to it. The phenomena of the world become here potential epiphanies.

It is difficult to follow the many diversifications of Buddhism, where the incarnation of Buddhahood takes manifold and endlessly repeated forms. In later Mahāyāna Buddhism, we are told, the male domination – which has diminished Christian institutions and perhaps played an oblique part in the furtherance of our recent onesided culture – has been relieved by the recognition of the feminine. This has occurred, apparently, not only in the form of the Prajñāgārumitā, the Mother of the Buddhas, but also in fostering in men the feminine in their own personalities. 'When they identify themselves with that Perfection of Wisdom they merge with the Principle of Femininity (Jung's anima) without which they would be mutilated men.'[1] This relation and completion is also portrayed as explicitly sexual.

The recent preoccupation with femininism in the West is in itself an accent on the castration of our lives by the cultivation of a part only of the human mind, and the entrenched power of a church organisation in which the feminine has no effective part – though this kind of attitude was not found in Jesus, nor perhaps in the very early days of Christianity.

The mutually interpretative roles of the inward and the outward are also present in Buddhism. – A similar stream within Christendom – neglected and often denigrated – has acted as a kind of preserver and conductor of the rediscovered insights which are stirring in our contemporary community. This is that underground stream already referred to which, through centuries, has kept alive for us in the West the possibility of today's changes.

For it is a plea of this work that for a Western mind to make an impassioned gesture towards an expansion of the meaning of incarnation, and a renewed recognition of its reality, involves acknowledgement of crucial changes in our recent narrowed conception of what is meant by God, and in our attitudes to time and space. It also involves a renewed accent on the significance of the inward life of mankind.

Deeply relevant to these explorations are those currents of meaning which reach us from within the more or less obscured areas of the Christian past. Here, we enter attitudes which bear a direct relevance to the present day, and to the necessity for a changed stance within Christianity if its meaning is to survive and to contribute to the human future.

In the medieval era the feudal society of the time presented dangers to the church (then the only conceivable vessel for the spirit), just as our industrial and technological society has done – but in our case at a point of history where the reaction to such danger is evoking from the western community *new* centres for the spirit which render the ultimate survival of the church in doubt.

[1] Zalpnes: *The Concise Encyclopedia of Living Faiths*, part 2, Wisdom. Hutchinson, 1977.

Within the feudal society the reaction was different, and severance from the church unthinkable. The recourse was to the revival of the monastic orders, which preserved the autonomy of Christianity and saved it from drowning in the forces of secularism. Monasticism in this style cannot be the refuge for today – nor an effective *reculer pour mieux sauter*. But some of the attitudes of monasticism find echoes in a revived emphasis on meditation and on the intuitive life. So that, in the 1970's we find Thomas Merton saying: 'In reality, the secular quasi-monastic movement of the hippies in America shows that the contemplative dimension of life . . . is definitely relevant to modern youth.'[1] He also says of the 'monk' in the modern world that 'he does not belong to an establishment. He is a marginal person who withdraws deliberately to the margin of society with a view to deepening fundamental human experience'.[1]

The hippies represented a flowering of protest that had its day, and was over. Its legacy is a rising movement that is at once less obvious, more coherent, and more widespread. It is in the context of this movement's increasing importance that we need to understand what might be called the underground legacy of Christianity which throws on our present scene an accent of continuity which is insufficiently realised.

Let us consider Anselm, an 11th-century Benedictine, and a prince of the church, becoming eventually Archbishop of Canterbury. He is famous for what is called his 'satisfaction theory', in answer to the question why did God become man. He saw the experience of Christ's crucifixion and its results in terms of God's recompense to the Son. This is part of the doctrinal questioning of the times. What is relevant for us today is not this kind of pedantic theological discussion, but the point where Anselm showed a kind of creative originality ahead of his time.

For he achieved a revolution in religious thinking whose effects were not fully felt until very much later. In his day there was no medium of thought conceivable other than within the confines of the church, so that the extent of his boldness was not present even to himself. The state of faith was for him simply the place where God induced in mankind as a very condition of human existence his own presence – this presence and not reason being the heart and essence of human thought. God can be known therefore without resort to authority. (Six centuries later, this attitude came to be the very basis of the Quaker faith, as it is to this day.) For Anselm it is in human existence itself that thought is born, and not initially in the processes of reasoning. Here is something, foreshadowed for us in existentialism, towards which the contemporary mind as a whole may be slowly moving. Implicit within it is a recognition of the impossibility of a denial of what we have called God. Such a conception transcends the limitations of all

[1] *The Asian Journey of Thomas Merton.* Sheldon Press, 1973.

31

religions. It defines for us what is human against the backcloth of what is greater than ourselves, and yet speaks within us. It is the birthplace of an unshakeable faith. God is in the world *in ourselves*, in the very substance of the mind and soul of humanity.

Roughly contemporary with Anselm, and more famous for the tragedy of his love for Heloise, we find the scholar Abelard preaching the necessity of doubt and hounded for it, becoming, in effect, in the end the father of the movement known as scholasticism within the church that condemned him. This was the opening of a horizon of reason, limited only by no relinquishment of the premises on which that reason operated, and which in the end destroyed it. But Abelard had said that grace was given by nature, and divinity was discoverable in the world, reflections which at that time were not to be tolerated. Yet, something was set in train. The immediate end of all this controversy was schism, and the world of the church started upon the road towards the creation of the general scepticisms of our own time.

Almost as famous as Abelard is the 15th-century non-monastic priest Nicholas of Cusa, who appears down the centuries as a figure of great appeal. Though this has been disputed, he has been seen by many as indeed a forerunner of modern times. Of his relevance to this moment there can surely be little doubt. Like Anselm, he too saw faith as beyond any formulation in doctrine, but there is in his pronouncements something of the quality we find in the pre-Socratics – a numinousness, almost an innocence. Cusanus's thought was overtly Christocentric, but, without his perceiving it apparently, it also carried him further. His search was for the hidden God, the God who, though he was in the world, was at the same time beyond the world. Cusanus's work has a beautiful lucidity, in itself persuasive. For him knowledge is impossible without that which precedes knowledge, since 'Understanding is the unfolding of what was wrapped up in faith.'[1]

He sees the universe itself as a trinity – 'There is not a being in the universe which is not a unity composed of potency, act, and the movement connecting them,' – and 'the beginning of a creature is due to God's being Father, its completion to God's being Son, and its fitting in with the order of the universe to God's being Holy Spirit. These traces of the Trinity are to be found in all things.'[2]

None the less, despite the orthodox imagery, he says also – thereby passing beyond the church's position on incarnation – 'Everything actually existing is in God, for He is the act of all. . . . Since the universe restricted is in each actually existing individual, then evidently God, who is in the

---

[1] Nicholas of Cusa: *Of Learned Ignorance*, transl. Heron. Routledge and Kegan Paul, 1954.
[2] *Ibid.*

universe, is in every individual, and every individual actually existing is, like the universe, immediately in God.'[1]

To Cusanus the godhead is *complicatio* (enfolding) and the world *explicatio* (unfolding). Later, we shall come upon something very like this in the work of the contemporary physicist, David Bohm.

Mankind is to Cusanus a second God – a human God – a second world, a microcosm of the whole – and what is visible is part of the invisible. (Here, we go back to 500 BC, to Anaxagoras of Clazomenae quoted in the first chapter of this book.) Such ideas are universal, and applicable to all human history including our own. God, for Cusanus, is 'the coincidence of opposites', and God's light is found in the darkness of ignorance. These paradoxes too seem to tremble towards those truths of mystical experience which are ineffable and all but inexpressible, and yet the same wherever they are found.

'A man', said Cusanus, 'seeking to see a light beyond his seeing knoweth that, so long as he seeth aught, it is not that which he seeketh. Wherefore, it beholdeth him to go beyond all visible light . . . And while he is in that darkness which is a mist . . . he knoweth that he hath drawn nigh the face of the sun; for that mist in his eye proceedeth from the exceeding bright shining of the sun.'[2]

This is an insight into the nature of knowledge, of awareness, which is the experience of all seeking human beings everywhere. Truth has to be sought, says Cusanus, 'where impossibility meeteth me . . . There, my God, art thou'.[3]

And in a profoundly incarnational vision, inverted as it were: 'when Thou, my God, appearest unto me as matter that may be formed, in that Thou receivest the form of whosoever looketh on Thee, Thou dost raise me up that I may perceive how he who looketh on Thee doth not give Thee form, but seeth himself in Thee, because from Thee he receiveth that which he is. And so that which Thou appearest to receive from him that looketh on Thee is truly Thy gift to him, Thou being as it were a living mirror of eternity which is the Form of Forms. While any looketh in this mirror, he seeth his own form in the Form of Forms.'[4]

He enlarges this by saying that the lion, if it were to attribute a face to God would see it as a lion's face, an ox as an ox's face, and an eagle as an eagle's face. Here, too, is an incarnational understanding.

Active in the practicalities of the religious life, this visionary priest supported, though this later failed, those conciliar theories which would

[1] *Ibid.*
[2] Nicholas of Cusa: *The Vision of God*, transl. Emma Gurney Salter. Dent, 1928.
[3] *Ibid.*
[4] *Ibid.*

have changed the practice of the papacy for which he worked. He sought a reconciliation with the Greek church, and worked continually for reform. He studied the Koran and recognised its affinities with the Christian scriptures. He recognised also that philosophy echoed in different terms what religion also said. He was interested in the science of his time and wrote mathematical works, was also a jurist and studied the humanism of his day. A man of great gifts, active in the world, he retained a devotional fervour almost simple in its power, and yet expressed with subtlety and with flashes of poetic insight deeply moving and charged with a perennial truth.

As the church began to emerge from schism, though Cusanus was active in the search for reform in high places, yet he had time to found charities for the old and the oppressed. If he speaks to our day – as he does for those for whom the poetry of his voice holds universal echoes – he does so as one who sees at the heart of the complexities of human living the presence everywhere of the divine. All that we know truly is, for him, charged with divinity. His thinking was symbolic, and reveals to our dessicated world the powers of the mind that we have neglected. Assailing the citadels of 'impossibility', he saw life transfigured.

The widespread rejection of such heights of thought as those displayed by Cusanus indict our own era. The symbols of the religious life in which he expressed such thought are in themselves a language. They are as relevant and as true to human experience as are the signs and symbols of mathematics. They are tools of the mind's activity as surely as are the lens and the plough the tools of the body's activity. Moreover, they are as closely bound to our daily life in its continual actuality.

Another forerunner in whom we may see the shadow of our present selves is Sebastian Franck (1499-1542), a Catholic priest. Certainly, in many respects he foreshadowed the Quakers – for he too reacted against the sole authority of the Bible, against external observance and the organisation of the church. A pacifist, he had no use either for religious condemnations. He asserted the presence of the divine in all mankind, and applauded originality of thought whether it was found within the church or outside it. For him, the Fall of man and his redemption were symbols of the eternal truths of human experience, and the true church was the company of all those who allowed God to direct their lives from within.

A more extraordinary figure is Giordano Bruno (1548-1600), a follower of the occult tradition of hermeticism, once ascribed mistakenly to Egyptian antiquity, but later seen to be of post Christian origin. What is interesting to us in Bruno is less his occultism than the scope of his general thought which went beyond the reach of his times. An Italian, and a dominican friar, he was in the end burned at the stake for his heresies. He may be called a Neo-Platonist, but his emphasis was towards divine immanence. He supported Copernicus, going further by envisaging the existence of many solar systems. He insisted also that there was no centre to the universe, that the whole of creation was one 'organum' animated by a world-soul, thus brilliantly anticipating some of the conclusions of today. The strange thing is that apparently he was condemned less for his philosophy or cosmology than for his refusal to accept certain theological dogmas.[1]

None the less in the occultism of the Renaissance there is also a relevance of a kind to today. The exercise of magical powers was seen as leading to the divinisation of man – through the marriage of earth to heaven by the action of man, not as the church saw him, but as 'Operator'. This road does not lead to incarnation in the sense in which Cusanus would have seen it, but has perhaps contributed considerably to the evolution of our dominance over nature, and the cul-de-sac we are entering today. The Renaissance Magus in general began the orientation of the Western ambition towards the manipulation of the world.

Yet we find Bruno himself uttering a poignant saying: 'For as the divinity descends in a certain manner in as much as it communicates itself to nature, so there is an ascent made to the divinity through nature'[2] – and this is directly incarnational. Bruno stands on the watershed between the medieval and the modern world, going beyond Copernicus in assertion of the infinity of the universe (an idea which is foreshadowed in Cusanus), and yet looking backward also. Bruno sought to 'bring the metaphysical down into the physical',[3] his aim being to relate the multiplicity of Beings to the All. His original Christianity was all but lost sight of in these exercises, and yet his mind was not truly modern and for him what reigned supreme was the internal power by which the mind of man contained all things. When accused, Bruno recanted and then withdrew his recantation. He was imprisoned for eight years, and burned as a heretic in 1600, the terrible fate of too many who have wished to extend the horizons of human understanding.

A formidable and difficult personality, apparently, he appears in temperament as different as possible from Cusanus, yet both speak to us with certain similarities, and with a relevance to our present conditon.

But of these and other figures of former centuries perhaps the one who is the most deeply and increasingly valued today is Meister Eckhart.

To read Eckhart today is not only to see him moving beyond the official Christianity of his times into a region of mystical exploration which is compatible at once with Buddhist and Hindu mysticism, with Quakerism, and with the searchings of the present-day that are rising within the

---

[1] David Christie-Murray: *A History of Heresy*. New English Library, 1976.
[2] Bruno: Spaccio Della Bestia Trionfante.
[3] Frances Yates: *Giordano Bruno and the Hermetic Tradition*. Routledge and Kegan Paul, 1964.

so-called secular community whose deep disquiets are leading them towards a new conception of the meaning of spirituality. The greatness and power of Eckhart are easily recognisable as outdistancing his religious contemporaries who charged him with heresy. He offers a vision of perennial importance to mankind's understanding of itself.

His imagery is basically Christian, but his use of it transcends the limited interpretations of the Christian church and moves into those realms of the spiritual imagination which go far beyond the limits of any particular cult. To listen to his language is to hear within his figures of speech a universalism of meaning. This, surely, is the action of religious language, of the poetry of religious vision, as it should be, and at its most creative.

That Eckhart was a daring thinker is evident. He has also been called difficult. If difficulty is a characteristic of excellence, then, yes, perhaps. But the approach to Eckhart itself demands that stilling of the self in the act of listening which is a part of the discipline of all contemplation. It is here that light dawns.

In the usual sense of the word intellect – not his sense – Eckhart's intellect was at home in the medieval world of scholasticism, but the coherence of his thought is grounded always in a kind of spiritual passion which at once transcends and illumines his intellectual power. He made full use of that wholeness of the mind of which our own era has so largely deprived itself. His loyalty to the church which condemned him cannot be questioned – but his vision went far beyond that of those who were set over him.

He was born around the year 1260, it is thought in a village called Hochheim in Germany, and he entered as a novice the convent of the Dominican Friars in Erfurt. Later, he went to the monastery at Cologne, then to the University in Paris, back to Erfurt, and to Paris again. His contemporaries were involved in controversies over scholasticism and the new enlightenment, but his own supreme concern was with the birth of the Word in the soul. None the less he became acknowledged as a capable administrator within the Dominican order, and when he finally returned to Germany he drew large audiences for his sermons.

Eventually, he became occupied in defence of his ideas both in yet more sermons and in the circulation of his writings. As far as they dared, his friends defended him on the score that he had been misinterpreted and that he had spoken 'from the point of view of eternity' (Tauler). In the end Eckhart's revocation was only of those aspects of his writing which had led to misunderstandings which could result in heretical beliefs, and not of their substance. Death may have saved him from further persecution. We don't know.

For Eckhart, 'When the Father begot all created things, then he begot me, and I flowed out with all created things, and yet I remained within, in the Father. In the same way, when the word that I am now speaking springs up in me, there is a second process as I rest upon the image, and a third when I pronounce it and you all receive it; and yet properly it remains within me. So I have remained within the Father. In the Father are the images of all created things.'[1]

This passage throws a brilliant light on that up to now largely unrecognised matrix of human expression out of which arose the doctrine of the Trinity. (Nor is a trinitarian conception peculiar to Christianity. It is also found within Buddhism, for example – the Trikaya – and in the Upanishads the supreme Brahman is represented as containing a triad.) Eckhart's words quicken the pulse of a human consciousness that is today reaching into depths of awareness unexplored before. What Eckhart reveals is the splendour, the all-embracing totality of the incarnated Word, *and its double action*. 'So I have remained within the Father' extends the meaning of Jesus's own words – 'I am in the Father and the Father in me' (John 14:11) – to the whole of mankind. Eckhart's statement also expresses with intellectual precision the action of all vision whether labelled religious or not. Here, in the 13th century, we find in Eckhart someone who leads us beyond the limiting walls of religious institutions into a territory we may at this moment be able for the first time fully to explore. Whether we do so or not depends on the strength of our response to the saving forces now rising in the world.

To all this must be added also a comment Eckhart makes on the Biblical text 'the Word became flesh and dwelt among us'. He says, '(always presupposing the historical truth of the text) . . . everything that is said here . . . is contained in and taught by the properties of the things of nature, morality, and art. The word universally and naturally becomes flesh in every work of nature and art, and it dwells in things that are made . . .'[2]

That 'always presupposing the historical truth of the text' emphasises the uniqueness of this medieval mind. Who else would have used such words at that time?

But the passage as a whole is remarkable. A return to this understanding – perhaps we should say, since such understanding has visited so few, an attainment to such understanding – may be the only saving direction for our chaotic world.

Eckhart says of God: 'He created the soul according to the highest perfection, and poured into it in its first purity all his brightness, *and yet he has remained unmixed*.' (my emphasis). This that is unmixed Eckhart calls 'the spark' (a word used also by the gnostics) – 'and this little spark is so

---

[1] Eckhart: *German Works, Sermon 22*, transl. Colledge. SPCK, 1981.
[2] Eckhart: *Latin Works, Selections from the Commentaries on St John 125*, transl. McGinn. SPCK, 1981.

closely akin to God that it is an undivided simple one, and bears within itself the image of all created things . . .'[1] Here is echoed, foreseen, a significance we find in the recent impact on spirituality of the contemporary scientific discovery of the hologram, to which we shall return later.

Expressed in the personal symbolism of the Father, the form of divinity which enters Eckhart's understanding contains intimations of presence and power that are yet to be fully elucidated. Perhaps they may never be so. For the ultimate reach of the mind of humanity is not simply incalculable. It cannot be measured in terms of calculation at all – but only in terms of vision.

The refusal of such vision is a blindness in the soul. Yet, in the end the very extremity of such a condition arouses within the human community those voices which are prophetic, and at first scorned – warners, summoners of change.

[1] Eckhart: *German Works, Sermon 22*, transl. Colledge. SPCK, 1981.

CHAPTER IV

The Voice of Prophecy

WHETHER REFUSED OR NOT, THE SENSE of God is endemic in the human condition, and no repudiation of the word itself can alter this. For the word God is a sign and symbol of the perennial presence within humanity of the impetus towards transcendence, which is the keynote of the life of mankind. Such transcendence is also affirmed in its negation – as life is affirmed in death. These corollaries, these opposites are conditional to one another. Similarly, transcendence implies immanence. The denial of incarnation is for mankind the denial of its own existence – nihilism. For the very existence of humanity is itself the condition of incarnation.

The justification for such statements lies in the history of the human race at those points where its progress between life and death differs intrinsically from that of the animals, who, strictly, have no history.

At all times, the concern of the prophet has been towards the urgency of the affirmation of God.

'The destruction of the God-image' said C. G. Jung, 'is followed by the annulment of the human personality.'[1] The threat of becoming something less than human operates half consciously, or simply unconsciously, on the alerted and often shapeless fears which today haunt not only the old but many of the young. The danger of nullity hides in the fabric of humanity's sense of itself wherever it has no reference point beyond itself. In this condition, that 'the centre cannot hold'[2] is a fear realised as continually imminent, as though in the vastness of the universe the extremity of the human condition has become no more than a disintegrating ball tossed to destruction by impersonal powers it has had the temerity not to acknowledge. By the denial of incarnation such a doom is evoked.

The function of the prophet is therefore the recall of the human person and of society to the sacred significance of its existence – that it is 'made in the image of God'.

[1] C. G. Jung: *Aion.* Routledge and Kegan Paul, 1959.
[2] W. B. Yeats: *The Vision.* Macmillan, 1988.

The achievement of personality is a part of this process. The movement towards consciousness evokes within the responses of the soul those divine harmonies which fill the universe – whose chords echo and re-echo within us, both as recollection and as attainment. For that which is beyond us lives within us and its manifestation is divinity visible within the world. For all men and women the power to discern this divinity is the gift of their humanity – and is independent of the agility of those trained mental powers which analyse, synthesise, and explore, revealing the hidden skeleton of the visible world, making out of this knowledge operable artefacts. Remarkable as these latter activities may be, their blind and obsessional pursuit contains a deadly threat – again, like that implicit in the Faustian story. We are a species among other species, made of the same molecules, but the awareness which alone differentiates us is the awareness that the presence of what we have called the divine pervades the living world.

There is therefore laid upon us the responsibility of celebrating its presence in rock and tree and flower, in animal, bird and star. The dominion over the earth referred to in Genesis is no more and no less than this. Prophecy is thus the voice of our recall to our own essence, and the prophetic imperative arises from an irresistible inward vision that is at odds with a denying outward circumstance. Consequently, throughout history the prophet is never a part of the current establishment, but one who appears an outsider, solitary, powerful – and the more powerful the more initially rejected. True prophecy may appear lost from today's chaotic religious world, and false prophecy visibly in the ascendant in those crudities of religious fanaticism which evoke and maintain disaster and war. For debased and reactionary forms of prophecy bring with them, eventually, destruction and fear. This has been visibly demonstrated in contemporary scenes in several corners of the world, as it was demonstrated in the aftermath of the rise to power of Hitler and the horror of the holocaust.

But the cry of the true prophet comes from those inner centres of awareness which creatively direct human experience rather than allowing it to drift at the mercy of every self-glorifying impulse and unsurrendered will. Its effects are dynamic and the fruits of its heeding set in motion those catalysts of change which transform the future. True prophecy evokes a change of heart and summons to a change in action. Without the prophetic call, no society can move towards change, towards a re-ordering of those elements in its organisation which are hurrying it towards disintegration. If the voice of prophecy incarnates the imperative of what we have called the divine, it celebrates and makes known the indissolubility of human existence from the primal ordering of creation.

In our own times such prophecy may sometimes take the form less of the individual voice than of the alerted group. For the power that has been canalized down the pages of history in the exceptional charismatic individual is entering upon a widening flow – and this is part of the coming change.

None the less, however it is voiced, true prophecy will recall us to the roots of thought that lie not in the centres of ratiocination but in the imagination – in the responses, the evocations, the soundings by which the soul of mankind navigates its journey. For the human mind is not simply a network of patterns laid bare in the physical structures of the brain. In its innermost depths it is a chamber of echoes, a cave of resonances. Here, the apparatus of thought dissolves into vision – into an immediacy of knowledge where one thing standing in the light of another throws on the soul an all-enhancing illumination. Here, and here only, the split in the Western consciousness may be healed. This is return – but it is also renewal. It is a return at another level of awareness to the early Greek sense of the seen as permeated by the unseen. It moves towards the future through the door of remembrance. The shadow of the past that we take with us explodes into light, as the seed-pod explodes into the scattering which is assurance of the bloom to come.

The prophet in our own time has appeared to move from the propitiation of the external god to the assertion of his death. But what has died is his externality. Are we now about to acknowledge at last the reality of his incarnation not externally, nor mediated, but directly, within ourselves? To re-recognise the presence of the god have we first needed once again to see him denied and crucified? For recognition comes when we behold him risen, and know that he is indestructible, not in some region of heavenly clouds of glory but in the living vibrations of the human soul. It is in the rejection of this knowledge that we move irretrievably towards death, and the whole world loses its luminosity, its transparency to the divine.

For the prophet recalls us to the reality of the human condition, which is never sufficient to itself. The encounter of the searching spirit is always with that which 'calls' to him – and prophecy is response to this call. The universe which mankind creates for its habitation is only viable within the integrity of its commitment both to itself and to what is beyond itself. It is to this double commitment that the voice of the prophet bears witness.

If the prophet is at first marginal, with the movement of time and response what his voice proclaims becomes central. The centre to which he returns us is that point where the creativity of the historical moment re-establishes a balance – achieves out of opposing discords a harmony in a new key.

At the hour of change the prophet of doom is as valuable to us as the prophet of deliverance. From Nietzsche, through Spengler, through nihilism, reductionism, perspectivism, the attempt to destroy the authenticity of the experience of the numinous has preceded the creation of that 'Wasteland' of the spirit which has haunted modern times.

> What are the roots that clutch, what branches grow
> Out of this stony rubbish? Son of man,
> You cannot say or guess, for you know only
> A heap of broken images, where the sun beats,
> And the dead tree gives no shelter, the cricket no relief,
> And the dry stone no sound of water.[1]

It seems fitting that this quotation comes from the pen of T. S. Eliot, whose 'view of tradition is historical' (Kathleen Raine), a fact which is plain also in his later and mature work. For his words encapsulate a despair that is caught in time. Whereas, when we move back in history to discover those individuals I have called 'forerunners' what they have to say, each in his historical moment, is in essence timeless. That is why they speak to us with an unchallengeable authenticity applicable to all times, whatever the idiom of their language. The words of the true visionary belong not to the temporal which is history but to the eternal.

After the Wasteland came those extremes of experience, the Nazi and the Stalinist régimes, the Second World War, the splitting of the atom and Hiroshima and Nagasaki. The voices of despair echoed for us in the prophecy that followed, in such figures as Camus, Mandelstam, Celan, Kafka. In these figures mankind expressed the need to *pray for God* – a prophecy acted out on the victims of the holocaust.

Out of the rejections of this bitterness, this intensity of suffering, has sprung a world geared to the cerebral, the manipulable, the superficial, the exploitable. Yet, deep below the visible surface, there is change, as though the very extremity of need becomes the catalyst of hope.

Thus, though it is true that the later despairs of our times have largely maintained a severance from tradition, and are uttered by solitary voices, whose use of tradition where it does exist is idiosyncratic and individual. Yet here and there we hear prophecy's authentic note, the summoning out of despair of a hope that is still half-Promethean and yet glimpses on the horizon the imminence of another vision. Thus, beyond Celan, beyond Kafka, beyond Mandelstam, we hear this voice, of the Hungarian poet, Sándor Weöres:

> But today some cradle rocks a fire-baby bringing
> divine gifts such as we hardly saw in our dreams.

> And just as in bygone days they laid open the secret
> strength of the material world: they will begin now to lay
> open the powers of the bodiless inner world.

[1] T. S. Eliot: *The Wasteland*. Poems 1909-1925. Faber and Faber, 1925.

In the hands of these children the lamp of reason does not
dictate, but serve; shining through sub-conscious life
forces & supra conscious spirit forces alike, illuminating them
and setting them to work in turn.

It was always others man conquered in the past; but – oh
tremulous hope! – in the future man conquers himself, & fate
subdues itself before him, and the stars.[1]

Such a voice echoes through the Wasteland of the present with a
nostalgia for a vision contained always within the forsaken powers of the
soul, as though the dim memory of these powers lingers despite their
attenuation – and tradition was reclaimable.

For our hope lies in our ability to break the prisoning shell of
information and acquisition that we have allowed to define our world, and
once again to see our lives as *ordered in the image* – that is, know once again
what it means to 'live in metaphor'.[2]

The image, the metaphor, expresses the scarcely expressible by which
we shape that towards which we move. It takes us into a level of meaning
where one thing seen in terms of another irradiates all things, affirming the
unity of the world. This is not irrationality. It is that supreme rationality
where what is seen and thought is brought into a presence within us that is
primordial. We have called this presence the sense of the divine.

Looking backward, we can see in the time of the Greeks, not only a
movement towards monism, but, for instance in Plato's 'Righteous Man'
who suffers for his condition a parallel to those figures appearing not only
between the Greek decline and the birth of Christ, but also much earlier,
who were claimed as incarnations of the divine. (It was even suggested by
Constantine and his contemporaries, and later, that the figure of the
Firstborn of the New Age in Virgil's Fourth Eclogue is a prevision of
Christ.) However that may be such incarnated figures are manifestations at
once of a tragic recognition and an unconquerable hope – of which merely
imperial divinities may seem a kind of travesty.

Our own materially orientated, pleasure seeking, and aimlessly restless
society has contributed to the decline of joy, the evasion of grief, the
perverted extraction from sexual life of tenderness and passion, and the
limitless ennui of the bored and cynical. We pursue 'knowledge', using the
surface ingenuities of our brains, and fail to see that the exposure of the
nerves and the supporting skeleton of any human organism has not touched
its essence. We have advanced to an acknowledgement of the validity of

[1] Sándor Weöres: *Difficult Hour*, transl. Edwin Morgan. Penguin Modern
European Poets, 1980.
[2] Edward Albee: BBC Television Programme, February, 1980.

43

'lateral thinking', but we leave the deep caves of the mind to an extraordinary abandonment.

If the present generation truly faces the imperative of change (political, intellectual, religious) out of which will come the continuation of life, it will see the appalling death threats of our times as themselves the intolerable forces which drive us to the creation of saving forms – and to proclaim this is in itself the action of prophecy.

For the new does not come from nowhere. It comes out of that darkness in which the thrust of the living, breaking seed is already felt.

So far, strength for the continuance of humanity has been always recoverable. It is so because within the spirit of mankind lies an awareness of the origin of his being in that greater Being which is creation, and of which he is an inseparable part. Behind the world of his sensuous experience lies a reality to which appearance is a gateway – and to this threshold the latest explorations of science are also bringing us. The sense of an ineluctable, terrifying, but marvellous destiny sustains the living human spirit, despite all.

The Greeks formed no creeds, issued no edicts that confined the imagination of man. They too sought to affirm man's affinity with the divine, evoking the gods of their own creation as arbitrary creatures that stalked the external world. But yet, at the heart of their vision lay an awareness that the search for truth is an *inward* search. They – who first freed the Western mind for what came after, both in its errors and in its vision – go with us on our further journey.

In a technological age which lives in a rootless present how is this inheritance of vision to be renewed – the sense of the past, not as something to which we seek to return but as the root of our present being, and as progenitor of the seed that we are under obligation to offer to the future? In the bankruptcy of philosophy in its recent forms, in the menace of a shallow, power-centred and irresponsible use of technology and an economic order maintained on a basis of successful rapacity, there has already arisen an uneasy, tentative, experimental turning towards the spiritual, (independently of organised religion which today follows, rather than initiates bold exploration).

Found in small pockets of inconspicuous communal or individual effort, this new movement includes an outward orientation which re-establishes the essential mutuality of spiritual insight and external activity. It recognises that the outward seen as existing exclusively in its own right is not simply deformed but ultimately sterile. Such a recognition establishes a forgotten imperative, that to maintain its viability earth must be informed by heaven.

This movement carries with it also a profound rejection of that deprivation of millions of human beings which is the cost of the material

44

affluence of the few. Equally, it carries with it a detestation of the mindless ravishing of the earth's riches. For the first time in history these considerations are emerging on a global scale, and the answer to the questions they raise is at last beginning to be seen to lie in the inward life of mankind. From this realisation the evocation of the prophet follows.

Here is centred prophecy and proclamation for today; as it has been centred relatedly on the Greenham Common women, on Bob Geldorf's initiative, on the testimony of the life and death of Steve Biko, and on the silent cry that fills the modern world from the insistent but hidden presence of the disappeared, the tortured, the forgotten. These are but instances of much more.

It seems that the emphasis of the new searching lies on a moving outward from former institutions, perhaps towards the establishment of more freely flowing groupings where responsibility is shared by all, irrespective of sex or race, and the corruptions of hierarchy and power are more likely to be transcended. The safeguard of these attempts may lie in a deep distrust of utopianism, which the realism of today has extracted from recent history. Experiment is going on, and here and there it surfaces.

In the direction of prophecy also we encounter once more the forerunners of our own day – those who authenticate for us not only the oneness of spiritual vision but its embodiment in that cry from the heart which recalls us to our forsaken destiny. On the historical outposts of the present day we may look back towards Jacob Boehme (1575-1624). The powerful note of his pronouncements touches continually a level of prophecy. Moreover, he, too, like Cusanus, Eckhart, Bruno, and others, offers insights of relevance to the searchings of today.

He was a Silesian, and a theosophist. Like Blake later, Boehme attributed his insights to divine illumination. He saw the whole of creation as the manifestation of God, describing the origin and structure of the universe in terms which included the occult, alchemy, and astrology. His language is the language of his time, heightened to a dramatic and proclamatory tension. He displays with fervour and conviction the timeless mysteries discoverable within Christianity, and the nature of God. The power of God he sees as the inextricable working out of both good and evil. His approach to evil has much to offer to the sceptical searchings of today. Evil he sees as the outcome of the self-differentiation of God, a distortion of the energy of God into wrath. The self-differentiation of God is an action inseparable from the creation of the world and the consequent irruption of self-will. In self-will are found the forces of darkness, confusion, and wrath. Not acceptable to the orthodox Christianity of his time, this attitude meets the rising insights into our own contemporary condition, where the non-integrated self pursues its own greeds and its own illusory satisfactions.

45

Also, three centuries ago, with a kind of foresight for this moment of history when conventional esoteric Christianity is losing its hold, Boehme said this: 'For Jesus Christ, the Son of God, the eternal Word in the Father (who is the glance, or brightness, and the power of the light eternity) must become man, and be born in you, if you will know God: otherwise you are in the dark stable, and go ahead groping and feeling, and look always for Christ at the right hand of God, supposing that he is a great way off; you cast your mind aloft above the stars and seek God, as the sophisters teach you, who represent God as one afar off, in heaven.'

The idiom of this passage is not the idiom of today, but the thought held in the idiom belongs to all time. It was the product of a revolutionary time, and of a mind ahead even of that revolution, which had been the result of a profound dissatisfaction with the reformation and which saw the birth, here in England, of the Quakers (who also affirmed the Christ as born, crucified, and risen in the heart).

Behind and within the Christian and alchemical imagery, Boehme's philosophy is profound. It is profound in the sense that it includes not simply theology itself in a deepening of the then current terms, but in doing this it includes also the inner imagination, the eye of the soul. Between the 14th and the 16th centuries religion and philosophy had become separated, and were to remain so, until now. But the vision of such isolated minds as Boehme's reunited them in terms, which, despite the involved language, are relevant now. For now the uniting of the whole of the powers of the mind has become a necessity for survival. The separation of the spiritual, the imaginative, from the 'rational' gave us in the end the dessicated modern age, whose bankruptcy has become so evident. Boehme saw the united working of all the forces of the mind as imperative, and all existence as subject to the 'consuming fire' of God, which is the liberation of its essence. For Boehme, evil is 'a dislocation of harmonised elements' (Hobhouse).

In a discussion between the enlightened and the distressed soul, he says: 'Just as a young plant is agitated by the wind, and must stand its ground in heat and cold, drawing strength and virtue to it from above and from beneath by that agitation, and must endure many a tempest and undergo much danger before it can come to be a tree and bring forth fruit. For through that agitation the virtue of the sun moveth in the plant, whereby its wild properties come to be penetrated and tinctured with the solar virtue and grow thereby. And this is the time wherein thou must play the part of a valiant soldier in the spirit of Christ and cooperate thyself therewith. For now the Eternal Father by his fiery power begetteth his son in Thee, who changeth the fire of the Father, namely the first principle or wrathful property of the soul into the flame of love, so that out of fire and light (viz. wrath and love) there cometh to be the essence, being, or substance which is

46

the true temple of God . . . paradise must thus spring up again in Thee, through the wrath of God, and hell be changed into heaven in Thee.'[1]

If the language of this imagery is penetrated by a willing understanding its phraseology, its unfamiliar colouration, is seen to be like the refraction of light from one medium to another – the light being the same.

Also, in a description which mirrors exactly the contemporary condition, he says: 'Every will which enters into its self-hood, and seeks the ground of its life form, the same breaks itself off from the great mystery and enters into a self-fulness . . . and so it is contrary to the first mystery, for the same is above all. And this child is accounted evil, for it strives in disobedience against its own mother which has brought it forth; But if the child does again introduce its will and desire into that from which it is generated . . . then it is wholly one with the same, and cannot be annoyed by anything, for it enters into the nothing, viz. into the essence from which it proceeded.'[2]

In these and other prophetic passages we encounter in Boehme a foreshadowing of Jung's individuation process, as well as an impassioned presentation of the essential power of a Christian imagery offered in unorthodox and uncompromising terms. Boehme's work is deeply incarnational.

The place where we stand today is already invoked in such voices of prophecy, recalling to us that internal world which is the core of our being – before which the unprecedented external marvels of our times are *in themselves* powerless. Are they so because both in the mode of their devising and the mode of their operation they are not incarnational?

One might ask, why trouble to read and understand a voice from the 17th century whose utterance, despite its power, may seem too complex for the untrained contemporary ear. Untrained that is in listening, within language, to cadence and echo. Perhaps the source of this poverty lies in an educational system which today neglects both the Greek and Latin classics on which our culture was founded, and also our own heritage of great literature. So that the contemporary ear remains untrained in responding to those intonations which in earlier centuries were apparently accessible to all, and which were charged with a depth of imaginative and emotional evocation that is absent from most of the communications of today. Too often we are offered instead the lifeless jargons of artificially separated and therefore superficial specialisations. In the production of the many 'isms' that litter the contemporary world there is a retreat from, a rejection of, depth of utterance. This is a part of that illusion of objectivity which

[1] Jacob Boehme: *Discourse Between Two Souls.* James Clarke, 1969.
[2] Jacob Boehme: *The Signature of All Things.* James Clarke, 1969.

imagines that language, castrated of its hidden but living power, can remain fruitful of essential truth. Acceptance of the decline and abuse of language is itself a sign of dessication of spirit.

The discipline involved in a total response to language is deeply rewarding, for it awakens within the mind an impossibility ever to be satisfied with the facile or the superficial. In reading a writer like Boehme the imagination itself is always engaged – as it is engaged also in the reading of another prophet for our time, William Blake (1757-1827).

The difficult figures of Blake's mythology are only difficult because they are renamed and given different appurtenances from those of tradition. But they are the same figures. They belong essentially to 'neo-Platonic, Gnostic, Hermetic and Alchemical'[1] traditions. As a company, they embody the archetypes of primordial human experience. Blake has links with the Kabbala, with Taoism, with the Vedanta, with Buddhism, and with Christianity – his Christianity diverging almost with violence from the orthodox attitudes of his times.

For Blake the figure he calls Los, equipped with the hammer of the smithy, is the spirit of prophecy, that aspect of time which in the human imagination is fused with the eternal.

Blake's prophecy laments the disturbance of the natural order within humanity. This order is fourfold. It is also the essence of individual mankind in its completeness. Blake maps the correspondences of human existence, and what happens when they diverge from the way of truth. The fingers of his perception touch exactly the contemporary condition and its loss of the symmetries of human existence. He found the images of his four Zoas, the basic aspects of mankind – reason, passion, imagination, and instinct (the body) – in the pages of Ezekiel. Because they are out of balance with one another, the four Zoas and their emanations are in torment. This is the core of that extraordinarily confident power which pervades his work. What it displays is the metaphysical truth contained in the full human condition by which he could say that 'All Religions Are One'[2] – something we are on the very edge of learning to say today. For him, his Christianity (Jesus the Imagination) was inevitably a part of the universality of human vision, and of the essential nature of mankind, which is directed towards Eden – that region of the spirit which lies beyond the duality of Good and Evil.

It is that same region of the spirit that we find in Cusanus, when he says 'Whence I begin, Lord, to behold Thee in the door of the coincidence of

---

[1] Kathleen Raine: *The Inner Journey of the Poet*, chap 4. Allen and Unwin, 1982.
[2] William Blake: *The Poetical Works of William Blake. Appendix to the Prophetic Books.* Ed. J. Sampson. O.U.P., 1928.

opposites, which the angel guardeth that is set over the entrance into Paradise.'[1]

Cusanus laid before us the immediacy of an attainable knowledge in which his own spirit was at home and over which he marvelled in an inspired celebration of its truth. But such figures as Boehme and Blake expose to us the inner significance of a Christianity stripped of unnecessary excrescences and exposed as an irresistible illumination within the living laws of the soul – in Boehme's case with an imperious prophetic fervour, and in Blake's case proclaiming the disasters of a situation where the wholeness of the human mind is dissipated. Today, are we at last alerted to the encroachment of such disasters? If Blake were with us he might well see ahead of us the first glimmerings of a horizon of hope.

The truly prophetic message is charged at once with immediacy and with universal relevance. It is this which demonstrates its truth. At a point of time it crystallises that timeless moment that is all moments – when the flow of the world returns upon itself, and at the centre of the whirlpool of existence there is discovered that immemorial stillness which is the eye of creation, after the manner of the eye of the storm. From this change is born.

A sense of the creative moment as always imminent haunts the human imagination. It is within this primal mystery where each moment becomes all moments that the vision of divinity has arisen. At the timeless centre it is pure – but nowhere else. Without the conviction that this purity is attainable, our humanity is lost, disintegrates. The sense of its attainability moves within our mutuality and is passed from generation to generation. It is the memory of our race, and sacred, its destruction the ultimate blasphemy. Out of the response to its imperatives has arisen within evolution the achievement of that individuality which contains also the whole – in a way that extends beyond the wholeness of the herd. So that the experience of loneliness becomes the condition of an awakened reciprocity of a kind apparently unknown in any other species to the same degree, and inseparable from the impulse towards the communication of transcendence. Thus, the connection between love and prophecy is profound, for it lies at the heart of the incarnational moment. The babe born in the manger offers its vulnerability to the incalculable and contradictory forces of life, and the wise men worship it.

But prophecy also throws up its stranger aspects – aspects which offer perhaps another perspective on to our access to what we call knowledge, in its fullness.

In the middle of the 19th century there arose a visionary teacher, Jacob Lorber, an Austrian. He declared himself acquainted with the fact that light

---

[1] Nicholas of Cusa: *The Vision of God*, transl. Emma Gubney. Salter-Dutton and Co. (1928). New York, 1960.

was an emanation of the rapid vibrations of atoms – long before such an idea was scientifically established. This same visionary foresaw, we are told – and with documentation – the then unknown secrets of the subatomic world, and also of the cosmos as we see it now. He foresaw, too, our world wars and our ecological crisis.

To appreciate this is not to begin to look for signs and wonders, or to enter the dubious world of superstition. On the contrary it is to acknowledge so far unexamined energies of which superstition is a degradation, as pornography is a degradation of the life-sustaining energies of sex. Are there antennae of the mind which can search out ahead of us regions to which only future generations will openly attain? Foreknowledge of various kinds, telepathy, and the elimination of the barrier of physical distance – these are some of the ambiguous experiences known to many of us. Today, research into what is known as the paranormal is at last beginning to be acceptable as a possibly fruitful activity, just as the brilliance of instantaneous calculation without the intermediate steps has been for long acknowledged as occurring.

All these questions lie within the orbit, so to speak, of the relativity of time and space. They serve to accent a probability of truth in the concept of the timeless and the timebound, the bounded and the limitless, the whole and the part, the good and the evil, as inseparable dualities beyond which lies that Whole to which only mystical vision has so far attained, and that fleetingly. But the act of imagination which conceives such states does not require that they be proved. Such an act of imagination freely passes into that region towards which all prophecy points, and which in itself does not seek authentication, since it appears to reach the threshold of Being itself.

The sense of incarnation is recognition of the concentration of Being at a focal point in which the Whole is mirrored. The frontiers of such recognition are today moving their boundaries, as the human consciousness is itself extending the area of its awareness into the very precincts of a rapidly changing science whose severance from the world of religion and of art is beginning to be seen as a dead end – worse, as an obstruction of truth, a kind of denial, that becomes in the end the crucifixion of the god.

The extension and the convergence of separated human attitudes upon one another lies at the centre of our cause for hope.

CHAPTER V

Convergence

THE QUESTION FOR TODAY MAY WELL be whether the course on which mankind has now started out – that is, a course which is a deviation from nature – is that of a false but recoverable destiny, or whether the fate of our audacious species is already sealed as moving not only towards its own death but also towards a total reversal of those impulses of creation out of which has emerged the universe that surrounds it. Moments of decline into brutality and degeneration have been a feature of all human history. But never before have we faced the possibility of the dehumanisation of humanity, or the danger of the artefacts of our own devising becoming our tyrants by abstracting human decision from the parameters of a shared network of responsible existence – substituting for freedom within the creative order obedience to the dictates of a mechanical and behavioural theorising which, in the end, traps and destroy the soul.

Today, we are driven to consider the inappropriateness of too much technology, of its blind pursuit – the devastating effects of the turning of agriculture into big business, of monoculture and the creation of dust bowls for quick profit, of irresponsible forestry conducted for the same reason, of the pollution of rivers and the sea and of food for wild creatures, of the inhumanities concealed in technological medicine pursued too far, of the ethical problems arising on every hand by the pushing of invention beyond the threshold of the moralities it can sustain.

The brave singing of a single bird before dawn will arouse memories of the glory of the dawn chorus as it was heard many years ago rising within the fields and woods of a countryside not yet grossly damaged, evocatively signalling the ending of the dark and the coming of day – for the relation of humanity to bird life has been in the past always poignant. Such signals now are abominably weakened, and at human hands. We fear for the whale, the dolphin, the seal, the creatures of the destroyed or threatened rain-forests, for the arctic wastes and for the heavens.

The memory of Chernobyl presents us with the blasphemy of the contamination of the very air we breathe, of the grass our animals eat, of the invisible corrosions that mock the pride of our power. For the driving force

51

of mankind's self-engrossed energies turns in upon itself and threatens to devour him.

Are we alerted in time – are enough of us alerted in time? Is there to these questions already a rising answer that will turn us from the exploitation that is the fruit of greed, from the deadly absence of love? Will the remedy lie in the recognition of the mutuality that sustains creation, in the lost recognition regained of the meaning of incarnation, of the expansion of this recognition into the darkened regions of the lust for transitory domination where the voice of the god is silenced?

The fragmentation of the wholeness of mankind has resulted in the obscenity of a damaged earth and air, a polluted sea and a space littered with the debris conjured up by the purposes of mutual destruction, a situation arising out of the concentration of power in unchecked hands – unchecked, that is, by the instinctual wisdom of that common man or woman for whom the loss of true humanity and the loss of relationship with the natural order would appear, simply, as a sin.

For the power wielded by the 'cleverness' of mankind belongs too dangerously to the few, is heady, and because of its so often blinkered existence within the laboratory, within parts of academia, within the centres of a narrowed political and economic domination, is capable both of a corrupt and of a naively destructive arrogance.

Yet, as the poison of violation increases, bringing with it violence, cruelty, fanaticism, and fear, within pure science itself, the science that is prior to the pursuit of technology, new insights are opening upon the vision of an end to fragmentation, of the possibility of a new recognition of the world as unified.

At this moment of sickness within a society on the edge of a realisation that it is threatened with disintegration, the future direction both of pure science and of human spirituality – and the relation between them – is of the first importance.

It is already evident that a revival of the sense of the spiritual is occurring outside and independently of religious institutions. This appears to be a spontaneous movement among scattered groups of individuals who are discovering *within themselves* a guiding spiritual consciousness. It is as though the insufficiencies and inadequacies of the Reformation are at long last producing a new revolution which acknowledges the inner reality of religious experience, not as something imposed from without but as a condition of human being itself.

This rising movement emerges as contrary to – and because of its creative content far more significant than – the parallel rise in escapist and reactionary fundamentalism which is one more symptom of threatened decline.

Perhaps the moment has come, therefore, when it can be generally realised for the first time that we must 'explain religions by the structure of man'. (Alain)[1]

This French philosopher would suggest that the essential structure of mankind has been the same always, and that this is the unavoidable context of change. (He did not live to see this context threatened as it is threatened now.) For him, as for many other thinkers, the movement of the human mind is dialectical, and if this is true, then departure from what is fully human disturbs the balance of existence, and does not further life, but death. Viable change must follow the contours of that which is changeless – which is one of the central arguments of this book – and the rootedness of humanity lies ultimately in a world that is given to him. At least, as far ahead as we can see, if change departs from that natural law which is the law of what we have called God, it becomes no longer viable.

Here, again, we come to Aquinas. To follow natural law is for Aquinas not a passive obedience but a *participation* in the eternal law which is God, and this free choice is the foundation of our humanity. For the eternal law is not imposed. What is required in mankind is response to its innate knowledge that the divine order *deserves* to be followed. This insight from the 15th century world of scholasticism touches the very core of the contemporary dilemma. It underlines the recklessness of the illusion that the *hubris* of mankind can be sufficient to itself – without God.

Does this mean that certain kinds of experimentation are forbidden – not from without by some remote destiny, but from within the very constitution of mankind, which carries within itself that spark of the divine in which creation originates. Such an attitude is incarnational in the deepest sense. It bears in its ultimate meaning an awareness that the divinisation of all things is the goal of existence – that not mankind alone but the universe itself can be seen to be transparent to the radiance of the divine. Where the sense of this radiance is fatally dimmed, life falters and is destroyed.

In failing to realise that we, the latest achievement of evolution, carry in our essential structure itself the developing awareness of the imperative of transcendence and immanence as one motion – latent perhaps in the animal and plant world – is to enter into a darkness where the ages-old direction of life is annulled. Is this perhaps tantamount to a refusal of life, to a movement towards the doom of yet another civilisation, but now on a world scale? If, now, the power that moves our life is to be recognised as within us, it is this recognition which will illuminate the course before us and save us from destruction.

[1] Alain: *The Gods.* Book 2. Pan. Chatto and Windus, 1975.

'. . . if I did not exist,' said Meister Eckhart, 'God would also not exist.'[1] A hard saying, but one towards which we move.

Are we losing that primal skill by which the hand that feels its way through the processes of nature, the creation of objects which express vitality and balance, and the care of animals within the bounds of their own needs, knows that the wisdom of its direction is fed from sources that lie deep within? It is this hidden direction which informs the coordination of eye and brain. The integrity of the mutuality of knowledge and action is sustained from this universal source by which eye, hand, and heart are guided. In return, the joy of labour feeds the spirit, and where this is so the cycle of creation remains unbroken. This is the experience of the artist, the craftsman, the mother, the explorer in thought or in body. It is the matrix in which the communal wisdom accumulates and pours over, is recognised and blessed.

In the noisy, stultifying, and crowding atmosphere of so many of the workplaces of today, in the ant heaps that are the large cities of the world, what remains of these attitudes? In the heuristic process, in discovery, what remains of that integrity of mind which refers each step, not to the excitements of apparently unlimited power whatever the outcome, but to those harmonies of existence by which every action and all effort is a mutuality?

Though in the Renaissance the bearing on human life of magical power was seen as leading to the divinisation of mankind (through the search of occultism for the marriage of earth to heaven) divergence from this route appears to have led in the end not to incarnational insight, but to our present ruthless domination of nature, and the consequent impasse of self-destruction towards which we are moving at a frightening speed.

If the revolt against these conditions is indeed beginning, then it lies not only in that instinct for life which is evoked by danger, but also in that rebellion against the suppression of what is truly human which arises when the god himself is denied.

We can turn here to one of the remarkable minds of the second century AD – Plotinus, a Greek born in Egypt and a neo-Platonist of great vision, a non-Christian whose influence on Christianity has been considerable. 'The effectiveness of prayer,' said Plotinus, 'depends upon a recognition of the facts of the universe.'[2] (This profound statement has a bearing, as we shall see, on the science of today.)

Is one of the facts of the universe the birth of the god within a mankind anchored in the earth so that the nature of humanity is indeed compounded

---

[1] Meister Eckhart: *German Works, Sermon 52*, transl. Colledge. SPCK, 1981.
[2] As quoted in J. M. Rist: *Plotinus: The Road to Reality*. Cambridge University Press, 1967.

of earth and heaven? It is the interaction of these two primal forces which can lead to their resolution in the One, the Whole, the All. If we can recognise that the sense of God belongs to the internal structure of the human spirit, if this can at last be seen to be so, then the significance of religion moves for us on to a new level of awareness. Perhaps only the power of such a conviction can be dynamic enough to avert the disasters that threaten us. Certainly, given such a conviction, we should then cease to need the localised cult – localised both in geographical space and in history – and a new era would have begun.

What is evident also is that a new era is opening up for science, and at the same historical moment, as though within the human mind a kind of climacteric has occurred. The new, experimental methodology within science which has followed on quantum theory, the acknowledgement of the relativity of space and time, and the attitudes of systems science, have begun to open doors upon the possible compatibilities between spirituality and science. However heretical and tentative as yet, such convergences may open the way to an expansion of the human consciousness, and the deadly split in the mind be healed.

Plotinus speaks also of a 'sympathy' between the various parts of the cosmos. How deeply striking is the similarity between this idea and those contemporary movements which in various directions have begun to converge on one another in the latest developments of human thought, both spiritual and scientific. These developments offer a way not only of mutual fertilisation but perhaps of salvation, for they see the universe as a vast network of mutually penetrating interactions. This bears a direct relation to the condition of spiritual vision.

Plotinus insisted that we start from the experience of our own reality. (To this stance the modern philosophy of existentialism has also brought us.) But if the experience of our own reality brings us to the acknowledgement of the spiritual (which may be described as the thrust towards transcendence) as an essential aspect of the internal structure of mankind – that without this we are less than human – then the question arises of the maintenance both of the integrity and the viability of our race where this imperative is denied.

It is at this point, which in itself induces a return towards those underground streams of wisdom which lie beyond and within the outward functions of the various religions, that we encounter within the newest explorations of science concessions to the essentiality of a kind of transcendence (seen in its own terms of novelty, of catalysts of change) fundamentally different from the idea of 'linear' progress.

Many unanswered questions arise here. But the mere fact that they arise opens before us depths of potentiality for the future.

If we say that the religious impulse is operative in every direction where the tools of communication are imagery and symbol and intuitive insight the medium of knowledge, then that is to extend the meaning of the word religion beyond the limited significance it has had as inevitably yoked to institutions, to specific doctrines and ceremonies. (This extension of meaning is the mark of the English Quaker today.) What we have called the spirit in mankind is expressed as radically in art, in literature, in music, in the action of love, as it is in what is specifically called worship. If we no longer need the focus of a cult, will the religious imperative become eventually a kind of suffusion within the activity of society, an awareness carried into every corner of life, maintaining the integrity of what it is to be human? This would seem a possibility.

But the question of integrity brings us sharply to the suggestions in the work of the systems scientist Erich Jantsch. Jantsch asserts that the work he describes provides a scientific foundation for what he calls 'an age-old vision'.[1] His work hinges on complementarity (the equal importance of chance and necessity), stability and instability, the unformed and the formed etc., and on a new vision of the dynamics of nature. In the natural processes of evolution, as in the human spirit, the key activity is seen as self-transcendence. In other words nature and culture are not separated processes, but one. This unified universe is alive, but its differences from the attitudes of traditional religion lies in the fact that its reference is only to itself. What is transcended is so within the potentialities of the created world. Does this bring divinity once more down to the hearthstone and into the heart itself? – but in a way inconceivable for those to whom the form of the god was not realisable unless given in an external shape? Here we are confronted with crucial questions to which there is as yet no answer.

But the actual consideration of integrity brings us sharply back to the philosopher Alain and his suggestion that we must explain religions by the structure of man. Here, we encounter in the scientist Jantsch the formulation of the idea of *auto-poiesis* as a property of living systems (an idea, we are told, originating in the work of a Chilean biologist, Humberto Maturana, in 1973 and developed by others). 'Autopoiesis', Jantsch asserts, 'refers to the characteristic of living systems to continuously renew themselves and to regulate this process in such a way that the integrity of their structure is maintained.'[2]

Accepting this, we see that it reflects our sense of imminent dangers and the argument of this work that what is threatened by disaster is the very structure of what constitutes humanity, in the rejection of those elements within him which define his spirituality. What is happening in the very

[1] Erich Jantsch: *The Self-Organizing Universe*. Foreword. Pergamon Press, 1980.
[2] *Ibid*: Introduction and Summary: The Birth of a Paradigm from a Metafluctuation.

56

revolution against this situation is a realisation that viable change must maintain the integrity of mankind *as* mankind. To become something other and less than human would violate those processes of nature which in the action of autopoiesis through the long journey of evolution have produced the essential human being.

Autopoeisis within humanity would mean then no severance from nature, but the maintenance of its laws. But Jantsch goes further in implying that the implications of the creative process itself lie within each created thing, exploding so to speak from within.

'The chances for true creativity,' says Jantsch, 'are seen in overcoming a dualism which separates the created from the creator.'[1]

In parallel, as long ago as the 13th century, Meister Eckhart said in one of his sermons: 'God's existence must be my existence, and God's is-ness is my is-ness'[2] (for which he was arraigned).

However, he says also, apropos of the 'breaking-through' to the divine ground: 'I receive that God and I are one'[3] – but God as ground is not here seen as creator but as primordial. We are therefore taken beyond Jantsch into a realm of inner experience which has been reached also at the heart of all contemplation, both Eastern and Western. This leaves a question mark as to what may prove to be, in the end, beyond the powers of science. In these directions facile and premature conclusions may lead us astray – so much is, as yet, veiled. If Jantsch moves nearer to religious insights than his scientific predecessors, he does not, as yet, move *all* the way.

None the less, he hints at it. The lost unity of the universe, (lost, that is, to the general awareness) he sees as rediscoverable since it is present within each self-organising system in the process of the unfolding of evolution. 'The highest meaning' he says, 'is in the non-unfolded as well as in the fully unfolded; both reach up to the divinity.'[4]

The word divinity is not explained, beyond a previous suggestion that God is the mind of the universe. But we can return here to Cusanus, for whom God and the world were *complicatio* (enfolding) and *explicatio* (unfolding). Where these two meet is for Cusanus the wall of Paradise.

Would it have been thinkable before this historical moment, at any time since the days of the Enlightenment, that the intuitive knowledge of a 15th-century visionary would meet so closely the implications of a post-Newtonian scientific enquiry? Perhaps it is not possible to exaggerate the

[1] *Ibid.*
[2] Meister Eckhart: *German Works, Sermon 6*, transl. Colledge. SPCK, 1981.
[3] *Ibid: German Works, Sermon 52*, transl. Colledge. SPCK, 1981.
[4] Erich Jantsch: *The Self-Organizing Universe*. Epilogue: Meaning. Pergamon Press, 1980.

significance of this kind of convergence, however tentative it may seem at present.

We find similar ideas in the work of David Bohm who uses the phrase 'implicate order' for that which is unfolded. Here, too, we are offered a vision of existence as one whole. David Bohm sees no break between the discoveries of the new properties of matter, which succeeded quantum theory, and the development of consciousness. He argues also that it is no longer adequate for physicists to 'engage in calculations aimed simply at prediction and control'.[1] What is needed is a cosmology which recognises unending process, in which our ideas of space and time are seen as abstractions from the deeper, enfolded order. (Cusanus's *complicatio*.)

Bohm believes too that intelligence and matter have a single origin, that knowledge itself is a part of a total process, that the universe is itself a harmony. (All these ideas belong also to a remote past, though they were reached by a different route.)

Bohm deplores what he calls the prevailing trend in modern physics by which the wider implications resulting from the theory of relativity and quantum theory are not faced, and emphasis is still laid on the atomistic idea of a universe of 'basic building blocks'. Pioneers like himself, in what might be called physical thought, are however breaking new ground, and increasingly. We may consider it significant that this is happening at the same moment in which we are seeing dissatisfactions with traditional religious attitudes, and a corresponding opening-out of the hidden and hitherto largely unacknowledged depths of meaning in what is called spiritual experiences. It is these still half-submerged but revolutionary forces which, in their resemblances, promise the ultimate emergence of a new order of thought, unified in both the inner and the outer world – where the roots of a 'new age' both of understanding and practice may be discovered.

In both fields we need for this purpose trained and disciplined intelligences alerted to potential discovery. But we need also sensitivity, discrimination, and a rejection of false trails. Above all, perhaps, we need hope.

Hope is derived from that inner surge of an affirmation of life that fills the mind and the heart of those who give up the self-assertion of the individual will (which is fragmentation), opening themselves to the entry of that grace which recognises and celebrates the unity of creation. In its contribution to the search for wholeness, revolutionary science seeks, in a new medium, an old wisdom.

[1] David Bohm: *Wholeness and the Implicate Order*. Introduction. Routledge and Kegan Paul, 1980.

What is grace? The descent of the dove (to speak in the language of imagery). The stirring within the soul of that divinity perpetually incarnated, crucified, and risen again – a divinity reflected also in every feature of the visible world. The idea of grace is still remote from scientific enquiry, but perhaps it draws nearer. For it is the implicate order, says David Bohm, 'that is autonomously active'.[1]

In an ingenious and involved interpretation of the latest hypotheses of science, David Bohm seeks to bridge the dualist gap between mind and matter, consciousness and the visible, tangible world. As a further progression into the implicate order, he postulates eventually an immense sea of cosmic energy which has been described hitherto as empty space (the void of the mystic?). Here, do we draw near to Eckhart and that divine ground which for him lies beyond the creator God? Or is there, in the comparison, a missing quantity?

Another point – using the analogy of music as a direct perception of the implicate order, should not Bohm perhaps have extended his analogy to what is contained in the image, in art, and in all poetic vision of the highest order. A consideration of language, of the 'word' follows later.

The scientist Ilya Prigogine suggests that we are witnessing the generation of a new dialogue between nature and man – but perhaps this dialogue has been perpetually present in forms other than those of analysis and overt elucidation.

Prigogine suggests that beyond the 'timeless world of supreme rationality'[2] previously sought by scientists there is 'a more subtle form of reality . . .',[2] and that we are moving out of a closed universe 'in which all is given'[2] into one that is seen to be open to change and innovation. Yet, for change and innovation to *be* change and innovation can they be realised except against the background of that which is changeless? Nor has a world of supreme rationality, outside science and certain philosophies, ever been what men and women have ultimately lived by, in any era of human history.

Reversibility and irreversibility is described as the novel element in quantum mechanics – but the simultaneous necessity of opposite states has lain at the core of certain kind of religious vision as a condition of all insight. (Height and depth are the same, said Meister Eckhart; also, evil is necessary to the perfection of the universe.) Does the intoxication of science with revelations of the complex workings of the structures of the universe, and their opening upon incalculable horizons *need* its balance in a metaphysics which also acknowledges new horizons – passing beyond the boundaries of positivism, reductionism, and, in the psychological field, behaviourism?

[1] *Ibid:* Chapter 7.
[2] Ilya Prigogine: *From Being To Becoming.* Freeman and Co., San Francisco, 1980.

Do we need the interpenetration of many formerly separated outlooks on the world in which scientific discovery is perhaps neither the only nor necessarily the dominant guide? If science is to reveal to us a dynamic and living universe in constant flux, our assent to this will come from the parallel working of an inner conviction which celebrates in the heart of continuous change an abiding power.

When Prigogine and Isabelle Stengers describe 'dissipative structures'[1] – the product of that disequilibrium which produces change – as displaying a 'coherent' condition where it seems as though each molecule is aware of the overall state of the system, whereas at equilibrium 'molecules behave as essentially independent energies',[1] are they describing also aspects of the general human condition? For it would appear that the mounting disequilibrium of our times is about to produce a new order by a drawing together of accumulating forces.

But when Prigogine and Stengers also say that 'the irreducible plurality of perspectives on the same reality expresses the impossibility of a divine point of view from which the whole of reality is visible',[1] from the stance of mystical vision this remark would appear gratuitous and unproven.

'The property of combining creative advance with the retention of mutual immediacy is what . . . is meant by the term "everlasting"'[2] said the philosopher A. N. Whitehead. In Whitehead we find acknowledgement also of that aspect of incarnation as yet hidden from scientific demonstration – 'the tender elements in the world, which slowly and in quietness operate by love'.[3] Has divinity entered the world of science as yet only on its speculative edge – leaving a profounder summons still ahead?

It appears to have been easier for some progressive Western physicists to relate their speculations to the metaphysics of the East rather than to Christian insights. This seems particularly true of Fritjof Capra,[4] in whom there is apparently no recognition of the significance of incarnation as it may be extended from within the Christian term of its focus on Jesus Christ. None the less, if it is through this channel, attractive in its apparent novelty, that eventually the parallel powers of Western mysticism will once more be realised and acknowledged after long suppression, then that will in the end be gain. It may release within the Western understanding a new conception that the concentration on the figure of Jesus is but the *direction* of the light – caught in a single lens but holding within itself the mirror image of the whole. A conception easier of general realisation since the achievement of the hologram.

[1] Ilya Prigogine and Isabelle Stengers: *Order Out of Choas*. Heinemann, 1984.
[2] A. N. Whitehead: *Process and Reality*. Part VII. Harper and Row, 1960.
[3] *Ibid.*
[4] Fritjof Capra: *The Tao of Physics*. Fontana, 1976.

What we have to explore now is perhaps that inner nature of mankind which lies beneath and beyond the pursuit of what has been called psychology. For the universe that we create is embodied within us, is perhaps drawn out from within us. At least, through modern science we are beginning to know that the line between observer and observed is blurred, that if objectivity exists at all it is at some at present inconceivable level of absoluteness. However, in the 6th and 5th centuries BC the Indian philosophy of Jainism had expressed an epistemological conception of relativity, that the utterance of any apparent truth is relative to the position of him who utters it.

Is it only by its incarnation that the Absolute (God) can be conceived at all? Might this discovery be a part of the message hidden within the latest scientific exploration?

Perhaps the new science of today is beginning to tell us, in effect, that we must return to the experience itself and not to the abstractions of theories formulated at one remove – that all things exist in a mutual involvement – that truth is unattainable except from within this involvement. Is it then possible for the work of science to become itself an exercise of hermeneutics in the sense in which the work of art can be said to be so? For the work of art is, in Plato's sense, recognition.[1] When science also can be seen as recognition will truth, for humanity, become one and indivisible? Indeed, science has already become recognition in the insights of a few of those of outstanding genius who know that the truth exposed by patient method is subordinate and subsequent to the truth of illumination – that the descent of the god is vital.

It is because of the descent of the god that the great art of any age can be said to be always contemporaneous. This, again, is incarnation, perpetually renewed. If the methodology of science is indeed changing creatively it can only be in this direction.

'The properties of the brain may provide the basis for religion and culture,' says J. Z. Young,[2] in a statement in which concession to other possibilities is found only in the 'may'. Yet it may be the impulses which result in religion and culture which determine the properties of the brain.

At least, there are contemporary scientists for whom the concept of numinousness has a probable reality, as it had long ago for Pythagoras (6th century BC), who believed that the key to nature lay in mathematics – number. It was he who discovered that musical intervals are expressed in numerical ratios.

[1] Plato: Phaedo 75.
[2] J. Z. Young: *Philosophy and the Brain*. O.U.P., 1987.

61

A contemporary scientist who approaches these questions in a way that recalls Pythagoras is Marie-Louise von Franz,[1] for whom the archetypal numinousness of number appears a reality confirmed within the microscopic world. She sees a living connection between crystal forms and Jung's archetypes, as though here the physical and the psychical meet in a common principle of nature.

These are difficult ideas, seeing number as a field of force, reinforcing in a new way the old idea of the music, the harmony, of the spheres.

Similarly, Victor Weisskop[2] asserts that the crystal reflects on a larger scale the shapes of atomic patterns. All forms in nature are based on atomic patterns, and the last electron added determines the configuration of the atom – one electron more produces a complete change. Weisskop suggests that the central force within the atom shapes the patterns which determine the behaviour of the atoms.

What is this central force? – we are left to ask. Is it that same creative force which we have called divine – and if science today is searching for a single force beyond the already recognised forces of gravity, electrico-magnetic force, and strong and weak nuclear forces, will that too become for us the basic impetus behind creation? Or are we to look further still? – to search for those hidden levels of meaning which have impregnated human life with a sense of a numinous, unknown, and primal power out of which emerges the achievement at once of the person, of beauty, and of love.

Where matter and spirit are assumed to have a common origin, the duality by which they have been seen as opposed disappears. Could this be a true form of transcendence for our day, by which we enter a new consciousness of the unity of inner and outer processes? Are we returning in a different sense to Karl Marx, for whom 'materialism' was the way in which matter thinks – the self-reflecting of thinking matter found in the human subject?

Do the latest suggestions indeed go deeper? At least they acknowledge the probability of a common matrix for physical and psychological forces. Is this enough? Can it embrace also what we have called the spiritual, and will there be a point where these hitherto apparently divergent routes meet and merge? If that is so, then what lies ahead of us could be at this point totally unpredictable.

Even so, the distance so far travelled already extends the concept of incarnation far beyond its original focus. When the idea, the sudden insight

[1] Marie-Louise von Franz: *Number and Time*, transl. Andrea Dykes. Rider and Co., 1974.
[2] Victor Weisskop: *Knowledge and Wonder*. New York, 1962. Heinemann, 1964, 1971.

which has been latent, becomes realised in consciousness, at that point the physicist Olivier Costa de Beauregard speaks of a 'psychisme incarné'.[1]

The search for what can unite the psyche in its subjectiveness with the eternal world is proceeding visibly. Will it come full circle, acknowledging that this journey has already been followed within that spiritual vision that has so far upheld mankind against all odds?

[1] Marie-Louise von Franz: as quoted in *Number and Time*.

CHAPTER VI

The Word

AT THE VERY HEART OF CHRISTIANITY lies an idea of such significance that it is applicable to human existence everywhere. This idea out-distances the working of that part of the intellect which is caught in the strangling web of reductionism. Its echoes penetrate far back into the chambers of a pre-classical past where to listen was to learn, to be emptied was to be filled. Within the organisations of Christianity this idea speaks with a subdued and often neglected power. Where it is authentically heard it marks a transition from the traps of conceptualisation to those forms of knowledge whose source lies at the very basis of human being, and which are supra-rational.

The cry from the Cross is the cry of abandonment, but it is followed by the words – 'into Thy hands I commit my spirit'. The interval between these two cries is the existential condition of humanity.

The involuntary cry seeks, asks, and in the end knows it is answered. It is answered by the offering up of human vulnerability to that which is greater than itself. This is the treasure, the Pearl of knowledge at the heart of Christianity. It is to this vulnerability, this courage to be exposed, this complete surrender of the abandoned heart, that truth comes as disclosure, in which the divine presence is revealed. To empty the self before the unbearable pain of human existence is to discover the reality of God as incarnate in our need.

An instrument of this neglected insight is the word – not the word of analysis, explanation, information – but the word as vehicle of that which is at once beyond and within, the expression of the unity of being and thinking. At the heart of humanity's understanding of itself, as at the heart of Christianity, lies the Word, in which the transcendent is brought into immanence.

In the 15th century we find Nicholas of Cusa speaking of our experience of the attraction of the infinite and how it engenders longing. Also (as with the early Greeks) that what we produce we discover. These are attitudes and responses which are, apparently, not dependent on historical change but basic to the nature of our being, through all change. If we had thought to

64

remake mankind in the image of his audacious bid for autonomy, we are now, today, brought sharply back to a realisation that the limits of that autonomy are set by Life itself. One instrument of this realisation may be the rediscovery of language, not as a mere tool but as a kind of fulcrum on which the whole human endeavour is balanced.

Our language, its meaning for us in the West, goes back inevitably to Greece, and to the enrichment of the spoken word by all that was made possible in the achievement of the written word. The horizons of the mind were extended by the subtleties with which language then found itself charged, the subtleties of anticipation and remembrance, of the conditional, of the possible and the potential by which the grammar of language shaped the mentality of men and women. This force was not subservient to events. It shaped them – and its power was enormously enhanced by the invention of writing.

'. . . that which comes into language,' says Gadamer, 'is not something that is pre-given before language; rather it receives in the word its own definition.'[1] Again, 'Language for mankind is not a summons to behaviour. It reveals to us the heart of our existence.'[1] If this is so, then understanding is not the product of a methodology but itself an ontology – and its manifestation is the word.

In our own day, the devaluation of language, which has corrupted and trivialised human communication, is an expression of the aridity that threatens us, and a part of our movement towards disaster. To realise the life-affirming unity of word and being is to enter into one of the deepest mysteries of our own existence. Through language we realise the continual flux of interpretation which is at once never-ending and also the foundation of all that we know ourselves to be.

In the Greek world the beginnings of the corruption of language lay perhaps in a reaction from the sense of its immense power as the vehicle of the numinous and as the carrier of a creative ambiguity at war with that clarity of mind which the Greek enterprise eventually sought. The Greek movement towards rationality demanded a separation between immediacy and the ideal. Thereby abstraction entered the Western mentality, and the Logos itself suffered a sea-change, so that in the end the image became a sign. In our day, language itself, outside certain largely obscured levels of poetry, drama, and religion, has become predominantly instrumental, contributing to that great impoverishment of the Western community which is now becoming slowly recognised.

The invasion of Greek thought by Christianity halted partially this decline in the understanding of the word. The Word of God heard as the fiat of creation became none the less something other than the Logos of the

[1] Hans-Georg Gadamer: *Truth and Method*. Sheed and Ward, 1979.

Greeks. It became an event, and its cosmological significance was transformed. For the event was incarnation. The phenomenon of human language carried now the whole weight of the meaning of God, and of the unity of the world under God. If the Word is *with* God, then once more language is recognised as itself within and not subsequent to thought. The truth of the word exists in its revelation of itself.

These complex ideas and symbols are for the most part passed by among those who have accepted Christianity without either theological elucidation or an understanding of the Word as demonstrated for instance in the prologue to St John's Gospel, and also in Genesis. (It would appear that the eventual literalism and the alleged historicity claimed by the Church is the source of this insufficiency.)

The life of language is anterior to, and greater than, the precision-orientated definitions of science. It is indeed living. It lives in its ambiguities, its metaphors, its myths. It speaks what is existent.

The animal calls to its fellows, and thereby induces a course of action. (Ernst Cassirer.) But, in a human being, language extends the horizon of experience beyond the location of the moment. It opens upon a world of experience that is unconfined in either space or time. It communicates the essence of a shared and extended life. For the Greeks experience became *aletheia*, an uncovering of a presence which reaches to infinity. This was the Logos. But infinity and the finite depend upon one another in a dialectical movement, and the strength of language is found here also. On this, Gadamer again offers a striking passage: 'Every word causes the whole of the language to which it belongs to resonate, and the whole of the view of the world which lies behind it to appear. Thus, every word, in its momentariness, carries with it the unsaid . . .'[1]

This action of language is apparent to all who work closely with words, not as instrumental to other processes, but as creative agent. All tradition and all history is contained in the revealing power of language, which reaches out also to the as yet unencountered.

If language and being were originally inseparable to the Greeks, have we now to rediscover this broken connection in terms that will relate both to the new revelations of science and to the re-evocation of spirituality? '. . . the technical term is a word that has become ossified,' says Gadamer, 'the terminological use of a word is an act of violence against language.'[1]

The jargons that have proliferated in recent years within various sciences – in particular, the social sciences and psychology – illustrate the life-denying attrition of language in our time.

In this connection, in the otherwise illuminating work of the scientist David Bohm there are passages relating to language in which he seems to

[1] *Ibid.*

present a distorted view. In rejecting the 'subject-verb-object' structure of sentences he advances the ingenious idea of what he calls the 'rheomode',[1] that is the verb rather than the noun as playing the primary role. He believes that this would avoid that fragmentation of thought which he sees as due to our describing what the world is rather than what it does. But the structure of grammar is merely the scaffolding of discursive thought. The heart of language lies elsewhere. The separations, the fragmentations, which have reached a peak in our time, lie surely in the discursiveness, the analysis, the delineations. What is limiting here is the constriction imposed on the mind by those faculties of the reason which separate in order to define.

This is the action of the surface activity of a language conscripted to the purposes of the classical methodology of a science orientated to the dissection of the world; whereas language in its fullness is itself a manifestation of life and being. Its total effect is unifying, and at the same time, because it is always ambiguous, two-sided, transparent, containing multiple relevance, it is charged with manifold meaning. The bearer of this process – which might be described as the poetic process – is the image, the concreteness of which is housed in the noun. It is the loss of the understanding of the image which impoverishes our thought, and is, itself, a loss of incarnation. This kind of thought is not sequential.

Though he does make apparent concessions to the poetic, language for David Bohm appears to be an instrument of ratiocination – whereas language in its origin and in its deepest manifestations would appear to be the creation in consciousness of that which already exists.

Under our expanding awareness of ourselves the form of the Word evokes acknowledgement as an evocation of the god who is incarnated in all the forms of the visible world. For the power of language opens before us a 'universe of truth' (Merleau-Ponty) which comes from within. The operation of language proclaims our existence as an existence which knows and forms itself. It may be said to do so because of the presence of God within the word. (There is as yet no form of articulation for these aspects of experience except in imagery – the imagery of the word, and also the imagery of the painting, of music, and of worship.)

The power of imagery is a part of the living experience of mankind, whether consciously articulated or not. If this process becomes totally lost to articulation we are in danger, and this is a part of the perilous position in which we stand today.

A year or two ago, a writer in a theological journal suggested that we need a Word Christianity which 'takes seriously the ontological function of

[1] David Bohm: *Wholeness and the Implicate Order*. Routledge and Kegan Paul, 1980.

language'.[1] It is precisely this which we are in danger of losing – above all, perhaps, in the opening computer age.

In an article in *Faith & Freedom*, the present writer expressed this situation in the following passage: 'The action of language is as basic to our bodily being in its relation to the world about us as the action of the five senses. Its operation is the product of the experience of our existence as an existence which knows and forms itself. It is a divination. Language is announced in our being. . . . To debase and destroy the word is to destroy ourselves, and of this today we are in great danger. The discovery of the revelation of meaning is not the solution of a problem or the accomplishment of a categorisation. It is a flash of being of which the word is the illumination. The light of this word opens upon resonances, upon a cave of echoes, from the whole of human experience. The word has the force of a gesture, is alive, secreting significance as the flower secretes nectar.

The multiplication of jargons, the decline of the word into a designation – this is the castration of language . . .'[2]

Of relevance here – especially in the direction of the meaning for one another of spirituality and the opening horizons of science – are aspects of the work of the scientist Rupert Sheldrake, though his theory of morphogenetic fields has been questioned. His hypothesis suggests a process of formative causation which can be related to the philosophy of Whitehead. Sheldrake's theory necessitates the repetition of modifying forms and patterns of behaviour out of which the current form has issued – rather than by the chance mutations of evolutionary orthodoxy. It appears to involve on the one hand a possible postulate of pre-existing eternal forms, and to that extent may be said to be Platonic. On the other hand the possibility could exist that across space and time the chemical and biological forms are repeated by a mutual influence of a kind not so far formulated. On this theory every event influences, and therefore in a sense creates, every subsequent event.

This theory appears to necessitate metaphysics – and has been given the name of 'morphic resonance'. It arises from the fact that material systems are now seen as dynamic structures and not as static substance. The morphic energy depends on the unity of energy and form which operates across the morphogenetic field. Its action has been compared to the dual action of the wave-particle in quantum theory. It opens the way towards exploration of what has been called the paranormal, for which the normal causal explanations are inadequate. It also brings nearer a conception of consciousness by which this is seen as in a sense prior to the motor fields

[1] William Gray: *The Myth of the Word Discarnate. Theology.* March 1985.
[2] Lorna M. Marsden: *The Transforming Word. Faith and Freedom.* Autumn 1985, no. 114.

associated with the body's physical states. Here is its bearing on the action of language, whose unity of form and energy creates its utterance.

Sheldrake's theories are problematic, but they do open a door that leads, apparently, *towards* the insights of the spiritual life in so far as these involve methods of communication outside the causal explanations of orthodox physical science. They allow for that interpenetration of the physical and the noumenal world which is the experience both of language and of all forms of art – and, supremely, of religions.

The action of consciousness on perception is a creative process in which the forms of language (like the forms of all art) – e.g. images, visual or otherwise, myth, metaphor etc. – are operative. This is Goethe's 'exact sensory imagination' which is governed by what we have called the spirit. (Ernst Cassirer.) The effect of these processes is not dependent on knowledge of their laws. It is an essential part of the movement of life as it is lived, whatever the degree of consciousness, by human beings. Sensational experience is a doorway to the creation of responses at a level inaccessible to the discursive reason, and here is the womb of language. The sign, (as in music) the symbol, is the irresistible medium by which alone significance appears to us – and it is fulfilled both in the moment and in memory. The sign which is language belongs to the unity of life in that it unites the inward and the outward. It is an energy taking form. Hence, the coming into being of a word *is* its meaning – and a form of incarnation.

The philosopher Herder (1744-1803), whose view of language, aesthetics, and history was organic, and who deprecated the attitudes of the Enlightenment, said of the word (as quoted by Cassirer): 'the first characteristic of reflection was the word of the soul. With it human speech was invented'.[1]

That is to say, the word is not an appendage to thought, but thought itself. In thought sensation achieves intuition. As Ernst Cassirer himself has put it: '. . . the word is not a copy of the object as such, but reflects the soul's image of the object'.[2]

The expression of Christ as the Word presents to us neither morality nor intellectual conception, but that which *is*. It is in this way that language presents to us, not the results of thought but the *presence* of thought. To lose this understanding of language is to destroy the roots of our awareness as human beings. The incarnation of our humanity in the Word is an existential truth which lives for us in the nature of our being and cannot be confined within the limitations, or the counterfeits provided by the institutions of Christianity. It is a mode of expression which can be understood far more widely. The cosmos is knowable to us, said Pythagoras

[1] Ernst Cassirer: *The Philosophy of Symbolic Forms*. Vol. I – (as quoted).
[2] *Ibid.*

in the 6th century BC, through self-knowledge. We can know the cosmos in so far as we are an expression of its image. In his prose work, the poet Coleridge wrote: 'Never could the eye have beheld the sun, had not its own essence been soliform (i.e. pre-configured to light by a similarity of essence with that of light).'[1]

All beings, says the Madhyamika system of Buddhism, have to be considered as God, and the manifestations of God are a free phenomenonalisation without limit. The Buddha may be incarnate anywhere and at any time. Also, in the Hindu Upanishads we read: 'The source of all names is the word, for it is by the word that all names are spoken. The word is behind all names, even as Brahman is behind the word.'[2]

This sacredness of the word, of the name, is a common feature of human understanding throughout history. It is another emphasis on the fact that language carries a numinous dimension far beyond its use as the instrument of mere speculation.

Very relevant here also is a passage in the Bhavagad Gita: 'The devotees of the Lord surrender unto Krsna and are thus able to understand him, but those who endlessly speculate remain ignorant of his true position.'[3]

If it is said that we do not live today by ancient scriptures, it is yet discernible that the uneasy contemporary mind is now turning towards those aspects of inward experience which are age-old, and is doing so in the context of the encouraging findings of the pioneers in present-day science. Moreover, the developments of such insights is revealing the parallels within all religions – thus giving to Christianity a hitherto unacknowledged provenance in the basic attitudes of mankind in general, a fact which surely augments for the unprejudiced the strength of its own basic insights.

Reinforcement for the idea that language is ontological, and not explained by analysis as a methodology, is found in the implications of some of the ideas of Wittgenstein. For instance, he asserts that the structure of reality can only be *shown*. Also, because language points beyond itself, the attempt to approach its meaning must be by the kind of understanding that we give to the work of an artist. In addition, since our linguistic practices have no objective support from outside themselves, therefore we must conclude that language is ontological. Wittgenstein on language brings us sharply back to the facts of experience, and away from those unfounded speculations of abstraction which try to treat language as an analysable system.

[1] S. T. Coleridge: *Biographia Literaria*. Select Poetry and Prose, ed. Potter. Nonesuch Press.
[2] *Brihad-Aranyara Upanishad*, 1, 6.
[3] *Bhagavad Gita As It Is* – Swami Prabhupāda. The Bhakti Vedanta Book Trust, 1968, 1972.

'When I think in language,' Wittgenstein said, 'there aren't "meanings" going through my mind in addition to the verbal expressions. The language itself is the vehicle of thought.'[1] Again – 'Every sign by itself seems dead. *What* gives it life? – In use it is *alive*. Is life breathed into it there? – Or is the *use* its life?'[1]

Writing in connection with language George Steiner says of Wittgenstein: 'There is a clear sense, persistent in Spinoza as it is in Wittgenstein, of the numinous as well as problematic nature of man.'[2] It is in this numinousness with which the heart of language is charged that the sense of incarnation dwells. We feel it in the Biblical record of him who was called the incarnate word, and we feel it also in the pulse that beats within the living exercise of language – in its evocations, its echoes, its resonances.

Steiner suggests also: 'It is via Leibniz and J. C. Hamann that language mysticism enters the current of modern rational linguistic study.'[3] But language mysticism and its acknowledgement has been there from the beginning. (It is always there in the voices of great poetry.) The 19th-century Humboldt described language as a 'third universe'[4] – the other two being the phenomenal reality of the empirical world, and the internalised structures of consciousness.

In his book on Deconstruction (which exposes what he sees as the limitations of the structuralists) Christopher Norris quotes Merleau-Ponty, from his later work *Signs* (1964), where Merleau-Ponty describes language as a 'surpassing of the signifying by the signified which it is the very virtue of the signifying to make possible'.[5] This is an illustration of Humboldt's 'third universe' in action, and a perhaps clumsy way of translating the original, but Norris also emphasises Derrida's conviction of the irreducibility of metaphor. He explains that Derrida's coined word 'differance' means that in the end there is no literal meaning, 'meaning being always *deferred* perhaps to the point of an endless supplementarity, by the play of signification'.[5]

How dangerously close is the method of such analysis to the prevalent aridities in the field of language which it seeks to remedy! Yet that the effort is made is enormous gain, and one more sign of those potential changes in which the renewed understanding of the meaning of incarnation may be attained more widely and more consciously.

In the attitude to these questions of the philosopher Heidegger, however, we find another note. 'The nature of language does not exhaust

[1] Wittgenstein: *Philosophical Investigations*, 1.329. Blackwell, 1972.
[2] *Ibid.*
[3] George Steiner: *After Babel – Aspects of Language and Translation*. O.U.P., 1975.
[4] *Ibid* – Humboldt, as quoted.
[5] Christopher Norris: *Deconstruction: Theory and Practice*. Methuen, 1982, as quoted.

elf in signifying, nor is it merely something that has the character of sign or cipher. It is because language is the house of Being that we reach what is constantly going through this house.'[1]

Of great significance to the consideration of the incarnational within language is Heidegger's discussion of the pre-Socratic Greeks in this relation. He points out that the Greeks had no word for language. Their Logos, which we translate as the word, is in its essence the being of all things. It belongs to the inseparability to the earliest Greeks of being and thought, of 'phusis and logos' – an inseparability so taken for granted that they never found it necessary to consider it. From this original unity, this wholeness, change could only be decline – a decline carried in our day perhaps to its furthest and most dangerous extreme, where language is so largely alienated from itself by the castration of its creative function into a mere reportage which so often issues in a lifeless and half-strangled jargon. (This is itself a reflection of the wider alienations of our disrupted society.) '. . . once,' says Heidegger, 'in the very beginning of Western thinking did the essence of language flash forth into the light of being'[2] – that is, among the precursors of Plato and Aristotle.

Heidegger's great concern was for the re-experiencing of Being as *presence*, a return within a modern consciousness to the fundamental experience of our existence in a mode of thinking which pre-dates conventional metaphysics, and in which the illumination of the numinous dimension of thought was taken for granted. Of this experience the word was the very breath. Its partial re-realisation within Christianity has suffered a kind of denial, a confusion, a renewed crucifixion of the Incarnated in which, now, the whole of our planet is involved.

As Hans-Georg Gadamer has pointed out, the incarnation of the word within Christianity gave to philosophy a new dimension foreign to Greek thought, in that the Word becoming flesh altered the cosmic significance of the Logos. Perhaps this was a necessary stage on the way to a further human self-realisation where the cosmic dimension is becoming returned to us in another form, out of the acute and crucial necessity to save both ourselves and the world. Once more, we may learn to see that 'the word that is true . . . has its being in its revealing'.[3]

'Keep in mind,' said Nicholas of Cusa in the 15th century, 'that in this world we walk in the ways of metaphor and enigmatic images, because the spirit of truth is not of this world and can be grasped by us only in so far as

[1] Heidegger: *Poetry, Language, Thought. What Are Poets For?*, transl. Hofstadter. Harper and Row, 1971.
[2] Georg Joseph Seidel O.S.B.: as quoted in *Martin Heidegger and the Pre-Socratics*. University of Nebraska, 1964.
[3] Hans-Georg Gadamer: *Truth and Method*. Sheed and Ward, 1979.

metaphors and symbols which we recognise as such carry us onward to that which is not known.'[1]

This approach is at the other extreme from scientific exploration, but its operation within the religion and the art of many civilisations makes the rejection of its validity an act of callowness. Reading the above quotation from Nicholas of Cusa, the contemporary mind in so far as it is blinkered may question not only the approach as a whole, but also the particular phrase 'not of this world'. Yet the metaphysical stance which has seen the existence of the sensible world as necessarily balanced by that which is beyond the sensible, is at least partially vindicated by the contemporary scientist's necessity to postulate the anti-particle, or anti-matter. For in the felt unity of the Whole – towards which the despair of the contemporary world is groping – the beyond is also within, and the apparent contradictions of polarity lead inevitably to their resolution in a unity which transcends them. This may be far from syllogistic logic, but it is the living experience of the freed imagination of mankind as it is encountered in men and women in whom Blake's 'doors of perception' have been opened.

Here in 1877 is Coleridge on this theme: 'In looking at objects of nature, while I am thinking, as at yonder moon dim-glimmering through the dewy windowpane, I seem rather to be seeking, as it were *asking*, a symbolic language for something within me that already and for ever exists, than observing anything new. Even when that latter is the case, yet still I have always an obscure feeling, as if the new phenomenon were the dim awaking of a forgotten or hidden truth of my inner nature. It is still interesting, as a word, a symbol! It is the Aoyos, the Creator and the Evolver!'[2]

Whatever selective respect we may have for the diverse work on language of such people as Whorf, Chomsky, Empson, Davie, Roland Barthes etc., yet to those who work directly with language as an art its generation appears organic, and incapable of elucidation in elaborated structures. (Grammar being but the scaffolding and not the building.) To the creative writer language is living. It moves within him like a creature in the womb, and in equal darkness, before it bursts into the light – when it leaps under his hands as the salmon leaps in the river.

In such experiences it appears that the significance of language lies outside the convolutions of the brain – as for Wittgenstein in the end the meaning of the world lies outside the world.

For two centuries and more science in its applications has set up its own conditions for the violation of nature, imposing on the processes of nature conformity to laws received as though these were absolutes at mankind's

[1] Nicholas of Cusa: Letter to Albergati, in 1463.
[2] Samuel Taylor Coleridge: *Biographia Literaria*. Selected Poetry and Prose. Nonesuch Press.

73

disposal. Now, we are beginning to understand that there are limits to the cultivation of techniques by which nature is violated (and perhaps also by which morality is violated). Abused and manipulated blindly, nature is rounding on us. Beyond the limited efficacy of the laws of classical science, we have encountered a realm of fluidity, uncertainty, ambiguity, interpenetration. A drastic change of perspective opens before us upon regions of the mind which hitherto have been outside the scope of science, but not outside the scope of the divinations of other areas of human understanding. It is in these other areas that language finds its truth, and the *action* of language cannot be equated with the rational framing of concepts.

If we have now the possibility of encountering in a hitherto apparently external nature the mirror image of the realities of our own internal world, such a suggested fusion is illuminated at every point by an expanded conception of incarnation in which the creativity of language forms for us our world.

If for the West, at this moment of history, the sense of the separation of the individual person both from the external world and from a remote divine omnipotence, is coming to an end, this is in part a gift of science to our day. It alters profoundly the framework of the idea of incarnation, expanding the meaning of the word so that the direct reference to 'flesh' becomes extended into a metaphor covering the whole of the visible and tangible world. This is the more easily received since we now know that the molecules which make up the flesh of humanity are the same molecules which make up animal and plant, tree and stone, and that the atom is an interchangeable agent contributing to the totality of creation.

At the obvious level the receding of divine omnipotence is one result of the decline of authority within the churches. It is also a result of the sense of the evolution of the world as endless process, in which the divine itself is involved (for instance, Whitehead's 'consequent nature' of God), and of the developing consciousness of a mankind no longer afraid of arbitrary terrors and retributions from without – newly aware that heaven and hell have no location in outer space, but exist, if at all, within the internal spaces of the soul.

Set formerly within the limits of its objectification, and thus requiring a mediator between earth and heaven, the idea of incarnation is now escaping from the net of its narrowed interpretation and moving towards the realisation of immanence, not as inevitably focused, but as permeating all things. Even the perspective of focus has changed. For the point in time is no longer seen as arrested, but as contained in its momentary wave within the continuous flow of all existence. The former boundaries have become fluid.

Against this shift of background the attempt to demonstrate the true nature of language as partaking of this fluidity is the more realisable. Language itself becomes a form of incarnation wherein what is transcendent moves within the utterance and announces the presence of the god as an irresistible part of its own necessity. What language mediates is this presence as a perpetual potentiality, as though the idea of immanence was illuminated from within its own operation.

Awareness of the working of this realised fluidity within language awaits its recognition in the extended consciousness of a mankind confronting either profound change or the possible death of humanity. The boundaries set within the movement of logic are a useful tool within limited purposes, but the essence of language escapes from such constrictions and can be seen as the evocation of our own becoming. The transcendent *is* the Word. Its descent is bodied forth within the ontology of language in a dynamic exchange by which being and thought inform each other – so that the world is irradiated by the divine presence within the inescapable mutuality of the action of all things upon one another.

This is one way towards the rediscovery of that wholeness which has been shattered by the splitting of the mind of Western mankind – and the consequent loss of awareness of the meaning of incarnation.

CHAPTER VII
Wholeness and Identity

WHEN WE CONSIDER THE VAST SPACES of the universe, or the sheer incredibility of existence, what anchors our thought that these confrontations may be bearable? If the individual life is a drop in the ocean or a grain in a waste of sand, what gives it the ineluctable sense of a powerful inner identity that is equal to the contemplation of the world?

In the ancient world the sense of identity was not clearcut, and the accessibility of the gods was balanced by their unapproachable otherness. This gulf was not the gulf between omnipotent creator and his creatures. It was the gulf of a similarity which carried a difference so great that any attempt to cross the divide between was futile, and the mingling of gods and men the usually disastrous exception. In this hardly bridgeable polarity the human struggle was caught. The route of escape became the cultivation of the rationality of the mind, and the conception of the city state. The effectiveness of the gods receded. The true god of the Greeks was perhaps the *Moirai* (the Fates).

Yet there is as it were hanging over the Greek mind the advancing shadow of monotheism. The dethronement of the Olympian gods, their relegation to the level of useful 'metaphors', left in the Greek mind an openness, an absence of any credal brake on the achievement of knowledge, and no edicts which constricted the free play of the human mind. Under the eventual dominance of the Stoic and Epicurean philosophies the central importance of the rationality of the mind was tempered by a contrasting emphasis on the operations of Chance. For at no point has that other route to knowledge, pejoratively described as irrational, suffered total decline.

There was abroad a conception that the soul of man partook of the divine life. That beyond the frontiers of reason the soul may be 'filled with God'. These aspects of later thought were strengthened by the influx of the Mithraic religion from Persia, and the revival of the Platonic idea of the Sun as the centre of the physical world. (Aristarchus of Samos in the third century BC actually advanced the theory that the earth revolved round the sun, but met with no support.)

With Neo-Platonism and Gnosticism the emphasis on the importance of the inward life was increased. The man who has 'known' God becomes the image of God, and, in some sense, *is* God. These ideas preceded Christianity, and they must have provided a fruitful ground for its rise. The prevalence of Redeemer figures offered variations on the theme of the saving of the soul sacrificially, followed by the glorious ascent to heaven. These cults were mixed with superstitions and extravagances, but their *direction* was single – towards the acknowledgement of the spark of God as incarnated within mankind.

The door was opened for the manifestation of the sacred history of the creation and redemption of mankind – Christianity.

Today, at the moment of a possible ending to what has been known as the Christian era, the questions of inward and outward, of immanence and transcendence, are beginning to return into those margins of the general consciousness where all change arises. But the emphasis is different, the context wider, the doom hidden within the activities of human life starker, the unmanageability of the world increased by the fact that for the first time in history the fate of mankind has become global – one fate. Moreover, a new accent has been laid on urgency – the urgency to discover, before it is too late, a route to the continued viability of humanity. The original spur to this urgency has been the splitting of the atom in a world in which the chaotic and persistent betrayal of spiritual and moral values has become an endemic danger, and the lust for power a more complex and more dangerous obsession than ever before.

Survival, ethics, spirituality – if these things are not gathered into one cleansing stream the world may have no future. The as yet half-buried awareness that this is so haunts the contemporary consciousness.

But the blind worship of technological achievement is over. Awkward questions are being asked as to the ultimate purpose of invention for invention's sake – or the appropriateness of ingenuities that may damage more than they relieve. There is also discernible the stirring of an acknowledgement that the pursuit of ever-varying possessions, and ceaseless economic 'growth' is producing not only the futile excesses of a uselessly accumulating litter (even in space itself), but also the depletion of the resources of the earth. In the West, a diminution of human happiness, of inner vitality, accompanies a kind of satiety that eventuates in a meaningless restlessness and in *anomie*. In less 'fortunate' corners of the world starvation and homelessness confront millions. Remedial patchwork is no answer to these problems. However, very slowly, in the obscurity of a half-ignored background, change is unobtrusively creeping forward and moving towards concerted action. In recent years these signs of change have increased very noticeably – for instance in the offering of economic alternatives or changed business strategies where the hierarchical order is displaced, where both planning and profit are more equally shared, where the importance of moral values is admitted, and where production for *need* is at least mooted. These attitudes are moving side by side with the tentative recognition that spirituality is not a dispensable epi-phenomenon or a sentimental luxury, but the ground of humanity's being.

If we are not to allow technology to subvert our humanity or to create a society that is enslaved by technological and economic determinism, we must recognise these emerging movements as aspects of incarnation.

In the last century it was the philosopher Schopenhauer who asserted that the greatest advances of physics would themselves create the need of metaphysics – moreover, that all we learn of the nature both of the particular and the general opens before us a continued mystery. In a remarkable passage, totally applicable to our present situation, he says: 'The inmost kernel of all genuine and actual knowledge is a perception; and every new truth is the profit or gain yielded by a perception. All original thinking takes place in images, and this is why imagination is so necessary an instrument of thought, and minds that lack imagination will never accomplish much . . . For indeed, if we go to the bottom of the matter, all truth, all wisdom, nay the ultimate secret of things, is contained in each real object, yet certainly *in concreto*, just as gold lies hidden in the ore; the difficulty is to extract it.'[1]

This, though Schopenhauer would perhaps not lay claim to such a reading, is an incarnational passage. Profoundly so, and not least in the phrase '*in concreto*'. In those words is hidden the perennial relevance of the figure of Christ, as himself an emblem of the truth of what we have called divinity embodied in the external world. To *see* this relevance is to extract the figure of Christ from the now stifling trappings of church history, and to see him as holding within his indestructible meaning the whole of humanity – and, by extrapolation, the whole of that creation of whose constituents humanity is an indissoluble part. In the identity of the single figure and our perception of it, in the 'minute particular', lies the whole, as it lies, visibly, in the hologram. In this process of recognition nothing is exhaustible. The mirror image recedes and recedes down the vast glass of existence, and is for ever repeated. The end is mystery, and if this were not so our lives would be unendurable and would sink into obliteration.

'We see our God everywhere –' said Coleridge. 'The Universe in the most literal sense is his written language.'[2]

Coleridge speaks also of 'a small water-insect on the surface of rivulets, which throws a cinque-spotted shadow fringed with prismatic colours on

---

[1] Schopenhauer: *The World As Will And Idea*, Vol. II, 1883.
[2] S. T. Coleridge: *Lecture on the Slave Trade*, as quoted in *Imagination In Coleridge*, ed. and selected John Spencer Hill, 1978.

the sunny bottom of the brook: and will have noticed how the little animal *wins* its way against the stream, by alternate pulses of active and passive motion, now resisting the current and now yielding to it in order to gather strength and a momentary *fulcrum* for a farther propulsion. This is no inapt emblem of the mind's self-experience in the act of thinking. There are evidently two powers at work, which relatively to each other are active and passive, and this is not possible without an intermediate faculty, which is at once both active and passive. (In philosophical language, we must denominate this intermediate faculty in all its degrees and determinations the Imagination. . . .)'[1]

As thus depicted in the parable of the water-insect the operation of the imagination contains the resolution of yin and yang, of all opposites, in the achievement of transcendence, the meeting point of heaven and earth.

It is in the working of the imagination that the self-experience (the greatest achievement of the evolutionary process) is itself transcended, directed towards the primal Wholeness. This paradox of an attained separateness as the only route towards an awareness of the transcendent All which includes both the self and the not-self is the ultimate illumination of spiritual vision. Its issue is the experience of love – oneness.

The generation of wisdom is found in the working of that creative perception which discerns the meaning of the world as hidden within the manifestations of the world. The abstractions of the mind convey to us the rules of the manipulation of the surface of things, the intricacies of structural organisation, or the mechanics of movement in space and time. But the reality of these externalities is affirmed only by what is concealed within them – by the unremitting obduracy of that which is not external and which for us has engendered the possibility of recognisable imaginative form. The consciousness of this double process moves in the human mind as the very condition of the viability of its own existence, and this is known in the instinctual life of all societies. Its articulation belongs to the long history of the human race. Its total denial would bring us to extinction.

Obscurely, the recognition of this situation is entering the gathering unease of many people in the Western world who have no formulation for what they feel, since the formulations of a no longer understood tradition appear to have collapsed beneath them. In these people the decline of religion has left a vacuum, both of imaginative perception and, secondarily, of moral guidance. The significance of the opening horizons of new scientific perceptions has as yet scarcely touched the wider population. There appears to be no sure path through the bewilderment felt in the imminence of change or the equal imminence of destruction. Only the antennae of the few are aroused, are probing the future with an increasing

[1] S. T. Coleridge: *Lectures on Literature, ibid.*

confidence that a new wisdom is attainable – that, once more, in whatever guise, the god will come down.

The dominance of the analytical mind is in the end destructive, for it cannot realise totality. Its fragmentations have destroyed that sense of the Whole which is the only justification of the part, its only provenance, and its only consummation. Methods of verification have been substituted for the face of truth which is many faceted, veiled, contradictory.

Technology operates in the region of 'signs' – and what has been called 'representations'. The heart-beat of human living lies elsewhere. A world order founded on technological expertise, 'profit', and aggressive dominance in the sphere of geopolitics, would be a world order with no living direction, ultimately doomed. (Deep structural changes in the organisation of the world are already being advocated, notably in two very different directions – that of the Overseas Development Council, and that of the recommendations of The Other Economic Summit (TOES).) The efficacy of our actions can no longer be judged within the limits of any one kind of operation, or by the equally limited expertise of any specialised section of society. Very slowly awareness of all this has dawned, is spreading. In effect, if not in name, it is a search for the encounter with incarnation – or the evocation of a forgotten Eros. Before the dawning of Christianity we hear its prophetic echo in Plato, speaking of Eros as '. . . a mighty daemon . . . for everything daemonic is the intermediary between God and man . . . so that by his mediation the universe is at one with itself . . . on one and the same day he will live and flourish . . . and also meet his death; and then come to life again through the force of his father's nature. Yet all that he wins is for ever slipping away from him.'[1]

Transposed, this not only points to the Christ figure; it is also Blake's Jesus the Imagination – that fire of the mind which is the crucible at once of humanity's creativity, and of its hope of salvation.

To seek new forms of expression of these things is not to alter their essential nature, which is the living nature of mankind – its estrangements, its reconciliations, the perpetually repeated tensions of its journey towards God.

Is it time now for a universal acknowledgement that the mediator whom we seek is no longer the external figure of the god, but the god within us? – That which is incarnated in the world, and therefore in ourselves, is a divinity whose image is active within the consciousness of mankind. For we have attained a freedom of the mind which through millenia has given to humanity a sense of the presence within the world and time of that which is beyond the world and time. The price of the long evolution of this freedom is our fateful choice of life or death.

[1] Plato: *Symposium* 202E, 203D-E. Penguin, 1951.

These pages have tried to present something of those forerunners for whom this moment of historical choice was already present, was eternally present; in whom incarnation was experienced, though not always so named, as an irresistible movement of the soul acknowledging itself as partaker in the divine essence. The word that we use, the power of language, is a sacred instrument of this revelation which itself passes beyond words.

Therefore the problem of human consciousness cannot be adequately confronted from the standpoint of rationality alone. Our awareness of life and ourselves is a total awareness, and the dominance of the rational recedes in proportion as we enter more deeply the flood of life. What keeps us afloat is the felt power in the flood that supports the skill of our swimming – for the sense of this power is there in all men and women, to one degree or another. So that the experience of life of the simplest peasant, or of the child, is no less valid than that of all the cleverness that disputes in schools of philosophy or that pores over experiments in the laboratory; may be more valid because there are moments when, without effort and perhaps without articulation, it sees further.

The philosopher Sartre quotes Merleau-Ponty: 'My body is caught in the fabric of the world, but the world is made from the stuff of my body.'[1] We are, to use another word of Merleau-Ponty's, 'enveloped' from the very first, not in what is alien, but in what is at once ourselves and more than ourselves. The world has no meaning except in the context of what is beyond the world, without which it could not exist. It is this beyondness whose habitation within us offers that paradox of our existence without which it would be inconceivable. Nothing in modern science can destroy this fundamental vision which has throughout human history accompanied our progress.

This chapter started with the question of our identity as persons. Over the last few centuries the development of a sharpened sense of separate identity has characterised the background to economics, to religion, and to aspects of literature. It produced a kind of pervasive liberalism, non-conformity, romanticism. In Europe both Fascism and monolithic Communism were in their different ways a reaction against this trend, but a reaction that has proved to be, historically, on the one hand shortlived, and on the other finally untenable. (This is irrespective of present attempts at revival.)

For all its limitations, medieval Christianity kept a balance between the communal and the individual. The instrument of this balance was the church. Its cosmology was a closed order. For the common man uncertainty was suppressed by an absolute faith that admitted no deviations and

[1] Jean-Paul Sartre: *Between Existentialism and Marxism*, as quoted.

presented a recognisable and unwavering dichotomy between good and evil. The responsibility for this balance of the two sides of man's nature was shouldered by the church.

Outside this bulwark of the communal soul, the questing spirit of mankind was not silenced but worked underground. In the present day these workings have issued in the parallel movement of astonishing scientific discovery and of a new spiritual restlessness. We are moving into an era of a hitherto unequalled uncertainty and of a totally changed cosmology. We are also moving into an era where the blind trust in an inevitable progress provided by science has been exposed as illusion. We are reaching a point where it appears imperative to recognise that the supra-rational faculties of mankind are unshakeably basic to his existence, that openness to wisdom must not only run parallel to the quest for knowledge but is itself primal. In this profound change the idea of incarnation illumines those processes of the spiritual life in which the individual returns upon the total, the Whole. It can do this only in the illumination of the interior life.

The astronomer, Bernard Lovell, has himself admitted that though a description of the state of the universe can be given in terms of nuclear physics and relativity, yet this is no more than a description. The unanswered questions that remain move perhaps towards the acknow-ledgement that 'there may not be a solution in the language of science'.[1]

In fact, in any consideration, a concentrated scholarship may destroy that spontaneity of response whose direction can be arrow straight. If indeed there is a movement of the newest science towards spiritual insight (or an attempt at the correlation of spirit and mind) shall we end by the celebration of this world not as irrecoverably divided from the spirit but as the only place of its unfolding manifestation? – and, in view of the above caution from Lovell, in what terms? In the menace of destruction which we have brought upon ourselves and upon the world has our sin been the rejection of the meaning of incarnation as central to our existence?

On the question of identity, of the person, we are returned to the image of the hologram, and to that search for wholeness which dominates so much of the progressive thought of the times. For, as we have seen, in the hologram the whole is envisioned in the part.

The rudimentary persons of animal life, of bird life are so often augmented by a reciprocal contact with humanity that our generalisations falter. Is humanity unique, not in kind but only in degree? The equation of intelligence with the highest forms of life is the result of millennia of human experience and the exhaustive effort of discovering in the apparently

---

[1] Bernard Lovell: *In The Centre Of Immensities* 7, Space, Creation and Comprehension. Granada Publishing Limited, 1980.

immense indifference of the universe a point where our vulnerability triumphs over itself. We have called this point self-knowledge, but it was first knowledge of the Other.

Out of the fracturing of our wholeness we have drawn, like the rabbit out of the hat, this Other who stands over against us. Without the fracture, would this have been possible? – and what exactly is it that we do to an animal when we encourage it, out of its puzzlement, to offer us something resembling love? Afraid of the word love in this context, we call it devotion. And what do we say to the visible nobility of the great tree whose years have raised its crown to heaven and implanted its roots deep in the earth? If we feel it as a *presence* is this arbitrarily to endow it with the apparatus of our own responses, or does it in fact communicate out of its essence the tremor of a life that is common to itself and to us?

Out of our divided soul we torment both ourselves and nature, and this is the obverse of that love that is at once too demanding and the inescapable product of our sunderings, our separations. Against this constant warfare religion has raised its bulwarks – and so has art. At this stage – and for so long contributory to our divisions – is science itself about to draw us towards those lost horizons where the divisions of the soul were born as a consequence of the act of creation? This moment is celebrated in the catalogue of the creatures in Genesis – but even science itself which has split the atom and measured the heavens, cannot elucidate the actual moment of creation. In connection with the projections within whose limits the comprehension of the universe becomes possible to an intelligent being, Lovell says: 'the processes of comprehension lead to an exotic, almost bizarre circumstance near time zero, where neither logic nor physical concepts, but only the infinities and infinitesimals of mathematics apply'.[1] He also asks the profound question whether 'there can be any reality in an externalised procedure for the investigation of an entity of which we are a part'.[1]

Biology too brings us up sharply against this limitation, stating that the stimuli which reach us are 'edited' by the brain. This selective barrier to complete information is, we are told, only missing in the simplest cells. If this is so, then we do not perceive the physical world around us as it is, as a totality, at all.

The awareness of such a limitation returns us, then, to those energies of the mind whose direction is internal – towards which this moment of history is already impelling us – as the only direction in which a forward movement may now be possible.

In this connection the psychologist C. G. Jung wrote earlier in this century: '. . . sooner or later nuclear physics and the psychology of the

[1] *Ibid.*

unconscious will draw closer together as both of them, independently of one another and from opposite directions, push forward into transcendental territory, the one with the concept of the atom, the other with that of the archetype.'[1]

Today, when the physicist is moving beyond the structure of the atom into expanding speculations on the whole nature of the physical universe, this prophecy is fulfilled at a new level – as nature and the human psyche are drawn nearer together.

Long before the establishment of depth psychology, the poet William Blake was aware of those aspects of the human mind which are universal. Mapping his vision of fourfold truth, he was aware (as, much later, Jung was aware) that when any aspect of the psyche is denied or takes on the characteristics which do not belong to it, then the order of nature is disturbed. But Blake's vision was cosmic. Our present situation provides a vindication of his warnings.

The sense of the human condition as a 'boundary' state between the angelic and the demonic belongs to a type of religious anthropology which is ancient and has been widespread in the East. It is a sense that is largely lost within the contemporary Western scene where the 'progress' of humanity has for long been seen as a condition of objectivism which is linear in direction. The possibility of emergence from this state is supported by the explorations of the world of the psyche which have widened their horizons considerably since the days of Freud. So that we find the psychologist Maslow admitting apropos the world of 'unyielding facts' as against the world of dreams and free association, that any assumptions about this differentiation 'does not deny that these worlds are related and may even fuse'.[2] This important concession has been followed up in the work of Assagioli and the theories of psychosynthesis.

These attitudes are exploring consciously those areas of human experience which for centuries have undergirded the more obvious manifestations of religion and of art – and which have been encountered, perhaps without articulation, by the matured psyche. That an awareness of the essential and indestructible reality of such inward experience is moving outward into the general community gives to our threatened condition one more light of hope. Endangered as a species, we need to know who and what we are in relation both to ourselves and to the world about us.

There are similar indications, too, in the world of neurology, particularly in the direction of individual identity. It is conceded by Alex Comfort, for instance, that our sense of identity 'patterns' the apparent

[1] C. G. Jung: *Aion*. Routledge and Kegan Paul, 1959.
[2] Maslow: *Towards A Psychology Of Being*. van Rostrand Reinhold Co. Inc. New York, 1968.

objectivity of the outer world.[1] In this connection too we enter the region of the aesthetic, where immediate recognition of a kind of harmony evokes a sense of consonance between the experiencing 'I' and what is known as the external world. This is not objectivism. It is a fusion, and it is instantaneous.

Alex Comfort would argue that human beings have a tendency to project their own responses into that which is not human, yet that this is always erroneous would seem to be less and less likely, as our knowledge advances scientifically towards that oneness of creation which is celebrated by religion. Here, we come again to the significance of the discovery of the hologram and its sudden relevance to the new directions of thought.

Alerted to the suicidal in the continuance of the blind manipulation of the world, we are realising anew that what is encountered in the depths of the inward life is always dialogue, and, in the end, interfusion. The self – the I – *enters* the not-self, finding there its consummation. The I which truly perceives knows itself to be inseparable from the perceived. '. . . the Father is in me, and I in the Father.'[2] That is an ontological statement as well as a religious one. In myth human action is portrayed as echoing what moves within the macrocosm, validating the unity of the world – the I holding within itself the mirror image of the All.

Within the psyche the I appears dual, as though there is an observer within the self. For this neurology has postulated a possible explanation in terms of a time-lag in the responses of the two halves of the brain. Yet this tentative explanation, though possible, does not penetrate beyond the structural. There remains, as always, the question of that creative impulse which has set structure in place – that command out of which creation arose, and for which we have no language save the imagery of the Word of command, and, above all and universally, the imagery of Light emerging out of primal darkness.

Creation is differentiation. For all the great religions of the world differentiation becomes the gateway towards that wisdom which is a re-possession of the Whole.

The answer to existence, the Sufi would say, is the liberation of the mind of mankind into that self-knowledge which returns it to an intuitive awareness that alone offers fulfillment.

Detachment and identification – the duality within the self – acknowledged, is resolved into freedom. This freedom is attunement to the world, to existence. The highly developed psychology of Sufism is not confined to Islam but would claim to be *human*. Jung himself has said:

[1] Alex Comfort: *Notes on the Biology of Religion*. Mitchell Beazley, 1979.
[2] *The Gospel According To John* 10:38.

'Psychoanalysis itself and the lines of thought to which it gives rise – surely a distinctly Western development – are only a beginner's attempt compared to what is immemorial in the East.'[1] The Sufi believes that evolution is now at the stage where humanity is producing new organs of consciousness activated by an inner mystical experience whose concentration has the effect of 'a centrifugal and magnetic force'.[2]

The mythology of angelology has accompanied the searching of the psyche – and also the hierarchy of heaven. The power of the Angel has entered not only the Bible but also Western literature, as the archetypal accompaniment to the journey of the soul. The Angel is the Other within the twofold face of identity. The Sufi, Idries Shah, quotes Ibn El-Arabi as saying: 'Angels are the powers hidden in the faculties and organs of man.'

In the non-orthodox Gospel of Thomas, discovered in Egypt in 1945, Jesus is reported as saying:

If those who guide your being say to you
Behold the Kingdom is in heaven,
Then the birds of the sky will precede you;
if they say to you: 'It is in the sea,'
Then the fish will precede you.
But the Kingdom is in your centres
and is about you.
When you know yourselves
Then you will be known,
and you will be aware that you are
the sons of the Living Father.
But if you do not know yourselves
then you are in poverty,
and you are the poverty.[3]

Whenever the road to self-knowledge is taken it is recognised as an inward road. It is the road to the discovery of the divine, the Whole, with which the world and ourselves in the world are suffused. Without the constant accompaniment of this presence how should we be aware that we exist? The creation of what we have called God is at once a necessity of our own being and an intimation. Of what? The answer to that question lies for ever before us. We search for it in our impassioned and evocative articulations, in our irresistible energies. We have sought for it in modern times in our conquests of time and space, of energy and artefact – but only its shadow is there. The Gospel of Thomas tells us that the outward alone is

[1] C. G. Jung: *Modern Man in Search of a Soul*. Routledge and Kegan Paul, 1983.
[2] Idries Shah: *The Sufis*. Doubleday and Co., New York, 1964.
[3] *The Gospel of Thomas*. Presented by Hugh McGregor Ross. William Sessions Ltd, 1987.

poverty, and the expanding horizons of contemporary science are turning in on themselves, are turning inward towards that microcosmic world where pure energy rules. What is this energy? Does it contain the intangible secret of consciousness as well as that of the dissolution of materiality?

In the language of that great visionary, Meister Eckhart, the Christ, who is the Word, comes to birth in the individual soul. The recognition of this incarnation, this epiphany, is the encounter with 'the Father', the All. But the form in which this knowledge is expressed is not dependent on the imagery of any one religion, or on those distortions which, within history, have overtaken the overt expressions of cult and ritual. At its uncorrupted heart each of the great religions expresses a single truth. In this truth may be hidden the ultimate secret of what we have called evolution – the cyclical movement of creation, going out from God, and returning into God.

The vision of humanity carries that impetus of creation which moves towards articulation, and, in the Sufi sense, to the unfolding of ever new and perhaps as yet unimaginable powers. The instrument of the realisation of this vision is the person in whom self-knowledge flowers. It is not by analysis that we reach this point, but by a kind of listening. We listen to the echoes within the soul which are raised by the encounter with the beauty and the suffering of the world. The evasion of this encounter is the denial of life. Its achievement crowns our existence with meaning, and opens upon a summoning mystery.

This kind of attainment has been the goal of all the great figures of the world religions – those who have withdrawn from the corruptions of power, authority, and elaborate cult – as it has been the spontaneous motion of the simply good. Each has sought in the depths of their own surrendered personality that Source which summons towards self-knowledge in order to transcend separation. The entire history of mankind is that of the secret progress of this irresistible journey whose meaning has been displayed on the screen of the world in dance and ritual, in the arts, in the elaborations of that cultic worship of which the Christian church has been one part, and in the artefacts created by the calculations and the labours of mankind. It is displayed too in the passage between men and women of the illumined glance, the mute communication of eye or touch whose unelucidated eloquence is charged with a vibrant power. On the treadmill of a totally externalised life these experiences appear lost, and the silenced harmonies of life descend into cacophony.

But, from within the hidden reaches of historical need the Zeitgeist answers the moment with the slow percolation of change. Hardly visible at first, such change gathers momentum. It is becoming steadily apparent in our own day, despite the backcloth of our appalling dangers. Whatever the clamorous leftovers of a dying era, the day has now gone when one religion can with impunity devour another in the name of the partial and clouded truth of fanaticism, when men can with impunity destroy one another in the now suicidal ravishments of greed and war.

This historical moment may be decisive for our civilisation. Under the malevolent energies let loose by contemporary mankind the threatened earth itself must receive the descent of the god in order that the remnants of his dismemberment may be gathered up towards a redemption of all life.

Today, the movement of knowledge is towards a new era in which our choice is literally between life or death. The key to a living future lies in the acceptance of our own destiny as inseparable from that of the planet on which we live, and the universe of worlds by which we are surrounded. Our immediate destiny seems to lie in a newly awakened participation in that dance of life which celebrates and affirms the reality of what we have called the divine – that inescapable lodestar set before us in the long journey of evolution.

To touch with truth the moment under our hand means to recognise equally within the depths of our own being and within the being of the world about us the ever-recurring presence of the god. His face is the face of that humanity which sees and knows him, and his form is the form of all men and women for whom the shaping of their own perceptions mirrors the evocation of a creative light.

CHAPTER VIII

Meaning and Need

IF WE HAVE INDEED THE SENSE OF AN inner identity that is equal to the contemplation of the world, the source of this sense appears to be found in those reaches of the internal life which lie behind and beyond the analyses of structure. The exploration of the brain exposes the network of its working, but not that which sets it in motion. Dissection, carried to the last extreme, either destroys what it dissects, or releases from it, to dissipate on the impious air, the phantom of its secret. The purely cerebral activity of mankind comes to a frontier where its arrogance, its *hubris*, is checkmated. It is checkmated by life itself, by the irresistible rise of those powers of the mind which have been neglected and disvalued by the contemporary Western world. None the less, the contrary motion to the worship of the analytical faculties may in its turn go too far. We see this today in the prevalence of fundamentalisms, the addiction to popularised forms of astrology, and the indiscriminate attention given to revivals of witchcraft, magic, etc.

The intellectual emphases of our society have been such that the extravagances of irrationality have received more adverse attention than the extravagances of the rational in isolation, pursued too far. However, genuine revolt against the over-emphasis on the rational exists, is increasing, and appears entirely justifiable. It has taken the form of a deepening awareness that the reality of spirituality, whose foundation is in the intuitive, is basic to human experience, and that without a recognition of this the deepest elements of the human psyche are castrated. Some of the effects of this castration have been demonstrated and discussed above – for instance, in relation to language, and to the neglect of the significance of modes of thought whose interplay takes place in imagery.

The revival of interest in religion is one symptom of these changes, but it is a revival, which, in its most vital forms, is apparently deeply *anti-* existing religious structures. As already suggested, it seeks the sanctions of spiritual experience in the constitution of humanity *as* humanity. Moreover, it sees the truths of the spirit not in one religion but in all. This is a change of far-reaching implications.

It is paralleled in the expansion of the frontiers of science towards regions where materiality dissolves into immateriality, and where the infinitesimal touches in its extremity a strange kinship with what is infinite. Here, in these heady regions, the notion of spirituality gains a new momentum, opens upon correspondences undreamed of, on possibilities which echo in a new medium the centuries' old wisdom of seer and visionary. The potential rapprochement of science and spirituality holds in the tensions of its struggling insights the possibility of a truly creative future. We stand on the threshold of a turning-point as great perhaps as that where the living organism first appeared.

But, as we cast our gaze backward in time, do we know the limits of what we have called the organic, the moment of change? Or are we to see in the whole sweep of evolution the inevitability of the emergence of that consciousness which exists perhaps in all things as potentiality? Elements of contemporary thought which see the earth itself as a living organism are filled with a new wonder, with a renewed and expanding awareness of the sacredness of the whole of creation, relating our own being not to a world elsewhere but to a cosmos whose integration with ourselves seems for the first time absolute.

'The earth is a compound mystery, for it presents us with the mystery of life in its entirety, the mystery of every individual form of life, and the mystery of ourselves and all our thoughts and works. (Since we are earth-made, investigation of the earth eventually becomes introspection.)[1] Here, again, is an incarnational voice.

Are we to be saved, at the eleventh hour, by that turning inward to which we can bring at last – at a point never reached before in our history – an unprecedented degree of self-awareness? Such self-awareness proclaims that our perilous identity is sanctioned by its inextricable validation in that encompassing whole which makes possible and supports its life. Without this whole, whose inmost aspect we have named divinity, our existence and the existence of the world would be inconceivable. The cry that is rising now, and becoming steadily more audible, is the cry against the insupportability of nihilism.

The artefacts of humanity – the embroilments of the contemporary world in the consuming activity of the machines we serve, in the artificially-lighted, air-conditioned offices where scores of men and women sit cheek by jowl with the computer and vast reams of paper, the highways built to the worship of a pointless and ever-accelerating speed, the crowded flight-paths dedicated to the same endeavour, the vapid ingenuities of commercial advertising and the prostitution to it of the skills of photography, the rapacious idolatry of money which itself has no solid existence as a product

[1] Jonathan Schell: *The Fate of the Earth*. Jonathan Cape, 1982.

of the industry of men, the accumulations of possessions far beyond the point of need, the evasion of maturity in those adult men and women whose leisure pursuits emulate, without the absorption and the joy, the activities of children – all these obsessive preoccupations sever us (and shield us) from that recognition of the strangeness of the world by which we know it to offer a transparency to what is behind the world. (The origins of philosophy itself, we have been told, arose in wonder.) From the demands of such recognition Western mankind has been in flight – and has taken with him, as victims of his own self-destructiveness, the comfortless millions of the starving and the homeless of the other half of the globe, as well as those among them who are emulating his own ways.

For the achievement of a form of living rooted in an awareness of the earth itself as the theatre of the divine manifestation cannot be separated from economic and political considerations. Visibly, we are coming to an end of the viability of the exploitative society, of the dominated and the dominating, and of the relevance to communal ordering of an outmoded 'class war'. The imminence of such change was foreseen by Herbert Marcuse in the 1960's,[1] and today we are witnessing the emergence of a new conception of the needs of the community which echo some of his ideas. This is visible not only in the converging directions of science and a reawakened spirituality, but in the steadily mounting repudiation of those competitive and aggressive values which require for their triumph the existence of the underdog. Despite the immense dangers and the endless cruelties of our times, there is a stirring of a revulsion of feeling towards a recognition of the divine image as stamped on all men and women.

For too long that peak of scientific skill and accomplishment which split the atom and thus exposed the secrets of matter has been handed over to a community incapable of supporting the burden, and the irrational temptations, of such knowledge. The unbelievable crassness of politicians supported by a deluded public has for too long eroded both the capacity for thought and the sense of our responsibility not only to one another but to the earth which bears us, which we have not only despoiled but are in danger of destroying. If reaction has indeed come, we do not yet know whether it has come too late.

These things haunt the imagination, and where they have been repudiated or ignored have gone about their destructive activity underground (as the warning of Chernobyl has so largely been driven underground) to issue eventually in violence, in alienation, in blind despair – and, in so many, in a terrible, futile acquiescence which is itself a repudiation of all that constitutes the value of humanity. In such circumstances the freedom of the personality is corroded, and the inner sense loses its directing power.

[1] Marcuse: *An Essay on Liberation.* Penguin, 1969.

There is perhaps another danger – a danger implicit in the picture of a crowd of men and women in a large and artificially lighted room sitting before machines whose operations not only dictate their lives but are directed towards an invasion of the autonomy of the human mind which would submerge its subtleties and its infinite variations. Is there a limit set to mankind's dependence on machines – not only by the erosion of that variation of personality and powers which is characteristic of humanity – but also by the danger of decay of unused faculties?

Or it may be that the projection into the machine will evoke its own limits from within the consciousness of mankind, as the projection into the externalised divine figure has done. Can the deviation from nature go only so far before it induces sterility within the soul, destroying that which is essentially human? For what is essentially human arises out of and is a part of nature. The discussion of the nature-culture opposition posited by structuralist anthropology appears now outmoded, not merely by the limitation of an analytical approach, which was always present, but, today, by the implications of a changed cosmology.

The supreme achievement of the advance of mankind appears to have been towards love, towards empathy, and towards the conception of integrity. The safeguarding of this achievement lies, not with the abstractions of specialists, but with the shared life of the whole community. What is required of us is the maintenance within our species of its true direction, and the wisdom to follow it as part of a total harmony. Our essence appears to lie in the embracing of a destiny that has been delivered into our own hands. To fail this destiny is to fail not only something unique in the world of this earth – it is to destroy a promise that is implicit in our very existence. From time to time this promise flames in the soul of individual men and women by whom it is mediated. It is a fire which we put out at our peril.

But the uniqueness of the human destiny carries also within its imperatives the fate of all the living creatures with whom we are surrounded, and the fate of the earth itself. Such a realisation is itself an affirmation of an inescapable truth – the inescapable truth that we, humanity, are made in the image of that God whom we have conjured from the depths of human tragedy and human hope. So, once again, we are brought back to the overtones of Genesis, and to the realisation of the metaphysical truth of incarnation.

But yet, '. . . need is one of the modes of our being.'[1] In that awareness which is a mark of our humanity we have brought this need to birth to a degree not known in any other species. If the sense of exile is endemic to humanity (and all our literature affirms it) then this is at once the source of

[1] Jonathan Schell: *The Fate of the Earth*. Jonathan Cape, 1982.

92

need and the promise of meaning. For there has come into existence in mankind that which has never been seen before, *the active creation of meaning* – and, with this, the evocation of an unassuageable need. Out of the realisation of need, of suffering, of loss, grows vision – and this is the message of the Cross. A new awakening to this message is an ineluctable part of an opening spiritual consciousness. We need to reappropriate the conception of pain, not as a negative experience which demands instant alleviation, but as an essential part of that creative dynamism by which the tensions of suffering and joy are resolved.

The deepest signals that direct our life arise in the imagination and the heart. The severance of cerebral activity from the primacy of the imagination and the heart leads into a desert of sterility where the ingenuities of mankind produce what is monstrous or without life. What is without life is seedless.

All the decisions that we take as though their putting into action had viability in isolation have in truth vibrations whose effects are limitless. This ancient visionary wisdom is corroborated today in the revelations that are offered to us from the activities of the latest explorations of contemporary science, where our world is now seen as a field of resonances, a pattern of inextricable interactions. To know this has been a part of that intuitive wisdom which for centuries has preceded, and now underwrites, the discoveries of the ratiocinatory mind which is now for the first time acknowledging its own limits. The long separation of the discursive mind from its roots in feeling and imagination has been yet another form of the repudiation of incarnation. For the god is formed in the womb of the soul, in darkness and silence.

The history of our time has had its share of that other darkness – the darkness of warning. If, today, we are moving towards the moment of repentance, of *metanoia*, how shall we read the poems of Mandelstam, or measure the heroism of such destroyed figures, countless numbers of whom are nameless? How shall we confront the memory of the holocaust, the firestorm of Hiroshima, or the pitiless uprooting and starvation of whole peoples in the name of acquisition and greed? The scale of such things meets at both extremes the scale of human grandeur and human blindness.

The warning concealed in such events is not met by an oblivious commercialisation of daily living or the setting up of the lifeless god of the indifferent marketplace. It is not met by the acquiescent anonymity of the crowd, or the posturing mindlessness of the yobbo. It is mocked in the battering racket of our modern cities, the nauseous fumes of their streets, and the futile exactions of a daily treadmill in which work provides the minimum of creative satisfaction except for the few.

'The urban by itself is impossible,' said Alain.[1] Behind the urban lies the remembrance of the powers of nature and their cathartic force. In the large, sprawling city disorder is not seasonal or temporary. It is endemic, and in our present cultural climate increasingly so. Yet the city is the controller of social order and the dangers of total imbalance release incalculable forces. Within these forces nevertheless the future is born – or there is no future. It is not the countryside that can itself redeem us, for it is already contaminated, but the places where thought moves – where thought becomes, in time, translatable into action that reverses chaos.

Even so, the threat of chaos is still answered by the presence of a single flower in the forgotten meadow, by the purity of a bird's last threatened call at evening, by the glance of love that passes between one human being and another, by the lifted head of the infant whose wondering trust is total – as it is answered by the hope engendered in the recognition by humanity of the perpetual impetus towards transcendence. The bearer of that impetus is encountered wherever the conception of incarnation grounds the earthly in the divine.

In beauty of gesture, in tone of voice, in momentary stillness, we feel the passage of that god who entered the imagination of our race as it began to emerge from its first darkness, discovering the soul. This is the treasure of our inheritance. The god is our creation. He is also ourselves.

'When man as image of God's infinity discovers the creative bent of his mind,' said Cusanus in 1435, 'he embraces the whole universe with it. Just as he is a second God, so he is a second world, the microcosm.'[2]

Cusanus articulated a new mode of thinking – that mode of thinking, none the less, which is concealed in the mind of the artist, the worshipper, the lover, and in the insights of the feminine, where, whether shaped or not, it is felt and known. It is a thinking which is at once more profound and more primal than the thinking of learning, and in our own day it has not been honoured. That we may be returning to a dim recognition of its power now offers us yet another source of hope.

After the illumination of an experience which came to him on a voyage from Greece, Cusanus wrote to Cardinal Giuliano Caesarini, 'I think it was a gift from on high, from the Father of Light whence comes all that is best, that I was led to conceive the incomprehensible in an incomprehensible way in the knowledge of non-knowledge, by going beyond (per transcensum) the indestructible truths as they are known in a human way.'

In these words of a 15th-century secular priest – words at the very margin of articulation – we may read an intimation of energies of the mind

---

[1] Alain: *The Gods*, transl. Pevear. Chatto and Windus, 1974.
[2] Nicholas of Cusa: *De Concardantta Catholica* II, 4.

which lie beyond our present horizons. Here is met the thought of the Sufi, mentioned above, who sees ahead of humanity the achievement of new organs of consciousness.

The mould of Cusanus's entire life was Christian. At that historical moment it was impossible for it to be otherwise. But his thought soared into regions beyond the limitations of any religious orthodoxy – and this, surely, is the point where we stand today, where the historical and cultural divisions of religious life can no longer contain us, and the insanities of a blinded 'secular' life are beginning to be seen as monstrous.

'If,' wrote Nabokov in 1947, '. . . the physical world could be said to consist of measure groups (tangles of stresses, sunset swarms of electric midgets) moving like *mouches valantes* on a shadowy background that lay outside the scope of physics, then, surely, the meek restriction of one's interest to measuring the measurable smacked of the most humiliating futility. Take yourself away, you with your ruler and scales! For without your rules, in an unscheduled event other than the paper chase of science, barefooted Matter *does* overtake Light . . .'[1]

That is deliberate hyperbole, but it states a possible truth. For we begin to see, over the horizon of present consciousness, attributes of the Mind where our sense of affinity with the movement and the meaning of Light imagery may be justified in ways beyond our present imagining. What awaits us may indeed be, at this moment 'unscheduled' within the present attainments of science but foreshadowed in spiritual vision.

'Why', said the heretic Bruno, in the 16th century, 'why, I say, do so few understand and apprehend the internal power?'[2] It was he also who saw pure matter as pure act, and conceived of a multitude of solar systems. That knowledge comes to humanity by ways closed to the discursive mind is a fact of human experience that is demonstrable throughout history, and its denial a complete and dangerous aberration.

The existence of hitherto unrealised pathways of communication is beginning to be mapped also within the hypotheses of science. In his discussion of 'dissipative structures', which follow from the fact of that non-equilibrium which opens the way to novelty, the scientist Prigogine suggests that such structures act as if each molecule was informed about the state of the whole system.[3] The relevance of such conclusions to intuitive communication may not be established, but the congruities are there. Recognition of the obstreporous intrusion of deviation into a world conceived as finally ordered must be extended to those modes of thought in which generalisation or categorical statement continually encounter their

[1] Vladimir Nabokov: *Bend Sinister*. Weidenfeld and Nicholson, 1960.
[2] Giordano Bruno: *From the Dedication of De Imaginum Composzione.*
[3] Prigogine and Stengers: *Order Out of Chaos*. Heinemann, 1984.

95

own limits. The complexity of existence does not permit the setting up of permanence in any kind of mental structure. Continually, contingency invades the illusion of inviolability, and this contingency is the herald of change. It has overtaken the separated religious worlds of our times, and has brought out of the darknesses of unjustified dogmatisms those constantly reshaped suppositions in whose depths are found a universal human aspiration.

One such supposition is clothed in the imagery of the descent of the god – a descent which is also an upspringing. '. . . the deeper the fount, the higher it springs; height and depth are the same.'[1]

When the scientist Sheldrake suggests the possibility of communication across space and time he speaks of a determination that is not *physical* in current terms. From the point of view of science his speculations move into disputed territory. Also, they evoke either Platonic Forms, or an impulse immanent in nature, or a transcendent creative agency. In the present state of science these attitudes are a summons to that acknowledgement of the necessity of metaphysics which we have already encountered. What they contribute without question is a reinforcement of the possibility that in the end a meeting point of scientific exploration and spirituality may be established in a region of the mind where the dissolution of materiality and the insights of the intuitive world discover a common matrix. This is a breath-taking prospect, but as yet far from confirmed.

At least, those tentative antennae which are already reaching beyond the borders of immediate knowledge offer the prospect of some substantiation for the idea of *meaning* as integral to the universe – or perhaps of regions of the spirit where meaning itself dissolves upon the infinite.

Our ceaseless compulsion is always towards that which is inaccessible to us. The tree is the creation of our seeing – so is the flower, the animal, the face of that other in whose lineaments we discover what we already love. Our love, like our sight, is the labour of what we do not know which brings to birth its recognisable similitude. Since it is gestated in darkness, why, and how, do we know that we recognise it? Yet we do know. The act of recognition is the spring of the soul and may be said to guarantee to us the truth of Paradise.

Without the anguish and the joy of these experiences what are we? On the vast mirror of the world the image that is returned to us is the image of ourselves – and at the same time the image of all things. The sense of the Whole that encompasses us is constant, though the noise of the world may appear to drown it.

[1] Eckhart: *Meister Eckhart. German Works Counsel 23*, transl. Colledge. SPCK, 1981.

These things are incontrovertible, for they do not belong to the time-bound domain of proof, but to immediacy. To shape them demands of language the utmost expressiveness, which is not precision but ambiguity and paradox. Can science learn to respect such approaches, to see how infinitely more they contain than can be housed in direct definition? For is this not the way that science itself is apparently going – towards a place where definition falters? What is required is a re-understanding that the word is creatively eloquent in its overtones. Perhaps the equation that is not resolvable, or the sign whose terms progress towards infinity may suggest the vortices of unanalysable thought and grant them the potency they undoubtedly contain. Are the shapes and patterns of these vortices repeated in the crystal, or in the vortices of water? We are told that the ultimate constituents of matter and of the psyche *may* be the same, and the possibility of an immaterial world coexistent with matter has already been postulated within science. (de Beauregard).

In these deep and uncharted waters the traditional forms that have been given to religious vision do not lose their truth but see the vessels of their expression broken and reassembled. The verity of religious attitudes is not confuted by the extraordinary reaches of the pioneering of contemporary physics, but rather paralleled. The god is still slain, in order that he may be distributed over the world, and miraculously reassembled.

When Jantsch asserts that 'the structure of DNA and the genes does not contain the life of the organism which develops by using this information',[1] by implication he is crossing the divide between a traditional dualism which saw the spiritual as irretrievably divided from the physical and those contemporary attitudes to which scientific reductionism is becoming impossible, and the evocation of the spiritual the likely direction of evolution itself. God, for Jantsch, is seen as the Mind of the universe.

Of all the forms that are given to God, is this less plausible than others? Yet – what is Mind? It is possible that there are reaches of insight to which the present conception of mind is but the threshold. The tensions that move within our apprehension of godhead are the inevitable tensions of the dynamism of our implacable searching, and our perpetual need.

It can still be said, however, that there is another route than that of science. This route is the route of surrender, of the passing of the soul into stillness, into those internal depths of the self where the Self beyond the self is encountered and the Divine ground is entered. Witnesses to this pole of experience are discoverable across the world and recorded history.

It is long ago that philosophy put forward the idea that knowledge is remembrance – that what we seek comes to meet us and is recognised.

[1] Erich Jantsch: *The Self-Organising Universe*. Introduction. Pergamon Press, 1980.

Largely lost sight of since the Enlightenment, this idea may yet be the guarantor that our inmost response is directed, that our need carries within its longings the promise of eventual fulfilment. If this direction is the direction of faith it is established by our diligence in the cultivation of expectation. This expectation dominates also the searchings of the scientific mind and is proof against both tedium and the momentary slackening of tenacity. It is another form of the same fervour which has raised our cathedrals and established the hierarchy of heaven whose peopling is by forms of the mind. Such forms are as veritable in their own shaping, and as grounded in experience, as the signs and symbols of mathematics. If they have lent themselves to distortion and literalism, to an externalised interpretation, has the hour now come when they may be seen as what they are, an assemblage of ideas and passions whose naming has given shape to what we internally long for? – and in so doing has offered this longing a validation. It has done this because in our achievement of such forms lies recognition of previsioned truth – faith being 'the evidence of things not seen'.

The expression of the nature of this process has found its perfection in one of the tenderest poems of the poet Rilke:

> This is the creature that has never been.
> They never knew it, and yet, none the less,
> They loved the way it moved, its suppleness,
> its neck, its very gaze, mild and serene.
> Not there, because they loved it, it behaved
> As though it were. They always left some space
> And in that clear unpeopled space they saved
> it lightly reared its head, with scarce a trace
> of not being there. They fed it, not with corn
> but only with the possibility
> of being. And that was able to confer
> such strength, its brow put forth a horn.[1]

Thus, the fabulous beast, the unicorn, bears kinship with – and inhabits the reality of – the gods. He too is an incarnation of that wonder by which the human imagination affirms the spirit.

That this affirmation does not share in the traditional rationalities of scientific explanation does not make it suspect, for it is also far distant in its operation from turgid superstition or mere fantasy. Its effects on the responses of the personality have created art, music, literature, religion. It reflects an activity that unifies, harmonises, and creates across centuries of differing history a shared vision. This is a vision of revealed meaning, of a

[1] Rilke: *The Sonnets to Orpheus*. 2nd part, transl. Leishman. Penguin, 1964.

profound awareness of the inextricable interpenetration of suffering and joy. It is charged with prophecy and power.

Are there in the latest hypotheses put forward by science tentacles that move in a related direction? We do not yet know with certainty – yet the possibility is there to a degree never experienced before. Contributory to its future elucidation is the sense of our world as itself the carrier of what we have called the divine. Within the world of contemporary expanding thought it is no longer generally implausible to postulate the power of the supra-rational as perhaps vital to the movement of evolution.

Within the supra-rational is contained the mystery of what we have called divinity, and its irresistible summons to the human spirit. This summons, which is the presence of the god, permeates the world. It also redeems the world. It is found in the simplest moment, in the moment of creative anguish, and in the rare moment of ecstasy. It contains a purity of recognition which is a promise – and the promise is of the actuality of Paradise. For this knowledge men and women have given, and are giving, their lives, in many quarters of the globe.

In the recognition of previsioned truth the movement of the human mind transcends the limitations of time. Within the latest explorations of science time is seen not as an absolute but as a dimension, a part of the continuum of a space-time in which the operation of the world is contained within our partial comprehension. Thus timelessness has entered modern science in a manner quite different from its earlier conception of the eternity of a fixed cosmos beyond the temporal world. The timelessness implicit in modern science moves towards an ancient wisdom which has seen the eternal as a necessity of temporality. The act of understanding crosses this apparent dichotomy, since in the act of understanding the doors of consciousness are opened upon the movement towards transcendence, which is the summons to becoming – being and becoming constituting the poles of our existence.

One may remember the devastating remark made by Democritus, around 420 BC, that 'many learned men have no intelligence'. Today, where learning (and the achievements of technological expertise) close the mind to the deepest movement of the human spirit, so that this is seen as superstition, our future is endangered. Our vitality as a species may well depend on our continued recognition that the unity of creation itself *speaks* knowledge. Such knowledge is open to all, learned and unlearned alike.

Beyond the world of relativity Einstein saw a timeless world that is coexistent with the timelessness that lies deep within the unconscious. For the philosopher Heidegger Being *is* time – and the recognition of being is also *aletheia*, an uncovering, a moving into presence of what is already there. The scientist Prigogine has stated: 'We are now entering a new era in the history of time, an era in which both being and becoming can be incorporated into a single non-contradictory vision.'[1] And Merleau-Ponty says: '. . . consciousness deploys or constitutes time.'[2]

Are not all these recent attitudes pre-dated and subsumed in the single phrase attributed to Jesus, 'Before Abraham was, I am'.[3]

It is the sense of the lost Paradise – in which is contained the impulse towards transcendence – that creates our need. It is our need that restores to us the assurance of the perpetual imminence of what we seek. This double action is the cradle of that meaning with which we have endowed our life, and without which we cannot endure. Meaning offers faith and hope. It is at once our own creation, and appears as a visitant from elsewhere. Its foundations lie in the action upon us of the glory and the tragedy of life. It is in the extremes of experience that the resolution of this contradiction is seen with starkness and we feel the vibration of life as at once a challenge and a promise of consummation. This is what we mean by catharsis – an experience in which meaning is affirmed on a plane beyond that of our daily round, to which we return changed, at once sobered and illumined. If there are wretchednesses of condition, or a pitch of destructiveness in which this experience is impossible, it is not the most extreme. Out of the horrors of the concentration camps, we are told, it was the good who emerged with their inmost selves intact. It is the good who have seen, either with simplicity or at great cost, that vision of meaning which is the human heritage, which cannot be totally lost as long as our humanity itself endures. Its perpetual embodiment is found in all the directions in which the impetus towards transcendence takes its many forms.

Out of a miraculous hope – that the transcendent and the immanent are one – the gods were born. It is they who are the guardians of the integrity, and therefore the viability, of our humanity. To deny them, to seek within humanity a self-sufficiency that expects the mastery of the world within the workings of the isolated arrogance of the human brain is to set in motion the forces of destruction and the decline of joy. Already, we are at this brink.

Now, in the tentative moving towards one another of science, philosophy, and spirituality, our vision of the whole cosmos is opening out, and with it our vision of ourselves. Within the movement of evolution, which is a single sweep, it is we who are the bearers of the self-realisation of that world of which we are an inseparable part, and to whose total workings we owe not only our existence but our apparently limitless potentiality. That which brought life out of the primeval swamp is the same imperative which moves within our consciousness. It is a call, a summons, whose

[1] Prigogine: *From Being to Becoming*. Freeman and Co., San Francisco, 1980.
[2] Merleau-Ponty: *Phenomenology of Perception*. Part 3, transl. Smith. Routledge and Kegan Paul, 1962.
[3] Gospel According to St John, 8:58.

ultimate meaning we do not know. But we have given this meaning an unfinished shape as the presence within ourselves and the world of that which we have called divinity. Whatever name it may be given in the future, it is not simply a guarantee of hope, but also of the continuing viability of a world in which the wholeness of an unfragmented mankind echoes in every part the wholeness celebrated in the sweep of a bird's wing, or the tremor of a tree under the passing of the wind. The sight through which our consciousness shapes the manifestations of nature, or the movement of the stars, is an *inward* sight. It contains the world as it is open to our perceptions. Out of that containment, miraculously, the god is born. Clothed in the flesh of our earth, he brings what is timeless into the time-bound.

This is the language of myth, of metaphor. It corresponds to the action upon us of both our being and our becoming. That which is beyond the world reflected in our consciousness dwells already within us, incarnated.

SI SONENT TUBÆ PARATUS